great WOMEN, great FOOD

PRESENTED BY
THE JUNIOR LEAGUE OF KANKAKEE COUNTY

great WOMEN, *great* FOOD

Presented by The Junior League of Kankakee County

Published by The Junior League of Kankakee County

Cover painting © by Jan Glazar

Photography pages 9, 27, 63, 115, 133, 151 © by Kankakee County
Convention and Visitors Bureau; photography page 97 © by Wayne Baranowski,
www.wayba.com; photography pages 10, 28, 46, 64, 98, 116, 134, 152 © by
Kankakee County Historical Photographic Collection

This cookbook is a collection of favorite recipes, which are not
necessarily original recipes.

ISBN: 978-0-9793614-0-1

Edited, Designed, and Manufactured by

CommunityClassics™
An imprint of

FRP

P. O. Box 305142
Nashville, Tennessee 37230
800-358-0560

Manufactured in China
First Printing: 2007   4,000 copies

Table of Contents

Dedication

Our cookbook, *Great Women, Great Food,* is dedicated in memory of one of our founding members and great women—Gretchen Charlton. Mrs. Charlton had a vision and resolved to form an organization committed to serving the community through voluntarism—not only to develop the potential of women but also to improve the community through the effective action and leadership of trained volunteers.

In 1976, she donated the Stone Barn to the Junior League of Kankakee, which serves as the headquarters for the Junior League of Kankakee County. The Stone Barn has evolved into not only a facility for our meetings, but also a melting pot where ideas for fund-raising and community service are formed. The recipe for success that Mrs. Charlton handed down to the Junior League was her way of "giving back" and striving to make Kankakee County a better place.

In her honor, we present this cookbook to commemorate her legacy, which, like a great recipe, can be passed down for generations to come.

Gretchen Charlton

Acknowledgments

The members of the Junior League of Kankakee County wish to express their appreciation to all the active and sustaining members for their recipe submissions, cookbook name suggestions, and other words of advice. The hard work of former League members led to the success of the initial cookbook, *Posh Pantry*, and we look forward to the success of *Great Women, Great Food*.

Great Women, Great Food is a tribute to the women of the Junior League of Kankakee County. It is a compilation of favorite recipes of our active and sustaining members while showcasing historical and treasured sites in our community.

Special Acknowledgments

The following people and organizations have allowed us to use their photographs to highlight Kankakee County.

Wayne Baranowski

Kankakee Convention and Visitors Bureau

Kankakee County Historical Museum

A special thank-you to Jan Glazar,
local Kankakee County artist, for her beautiful
painting on the front cover.

Committee

Chairman—Sherri Lockman-Crawford

Co-Chairman—Lesley Robinson

Sarah Bowman-Steffes

Leslie Geoffrey

Karen Johnston-Gentry

Jane Koehler

Jackie Ludwig

Mission Statement

The Junior League of Kankakee County is an organization of
women committed to promoting voluntarism, developing the
potential of women, and improving the community through the
effective action and leadership of trained volunteers. Its purpose
is exclusively educational and charitable.

Brunch and Breads

The famous **Red Barn**

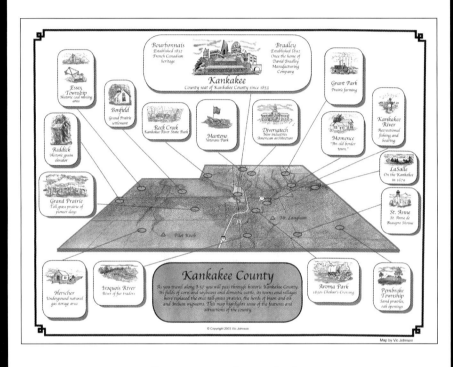

Bourbonnais
Established 1832
French Canadian
heritage

Bradley
Established 1892
Once the home of
David Bradley
Manufacturing
Company

Kankakee
County seat of Kankakee County since 1853

Essex
Township
Historic coal mining
area

Grant Park
Prairie farming

Bonfield
Grand Prairie
settlement

Rock Creek
Kankakee River State Park

Manteno
Veterans Park

Diversatech
New industries
American architecture

Momence
"An old border
town."

Kankakee
River
Recreational
fishing and
boating

Reddick
Historic grain
elevator

LaSalle
On the Kankakee
in 1679

Grand Prairie
Tall grass prairie of
pioneer days

St. Anne
St. Anne de
Beaupre Shrine

Mt. Langham

Pilot Knob

Herscher
Underground natural
gas storage area

Iroquois River
River of fur traders

Kankakee County

As you travel along I-57 you will pass through historic Kankakee County.
Its fields of corn and soybeans and domestic cattle, its towns and villages
have replaced the once tall grass prairies, the herds of bison and elk
and Indian wigwams. This map highlights some of the features and
attractions of the county.

Aroma Park
1830s Chebar's Crossing

Pembroke
Township
Sand prairies,
oak openings

The Map of Kankakee

Spinach and Onion Quiche

1 onion, chopped
3 tablespoons butter or margarine
3 eggs
1 cup heavy cream
1/2 cup (2 ounces) grated Parmesan cheese
1/2 cup (2 ounces) shredded cheese
1/4 teaspoon hot red pepper sauce
1 envelope ranch salad dressing mix
1 (10-ounce) package frozen spinach,
    thawed and drained
1 baked (9-inch) pie shell, cooled

Sauté the onion in the butter in a medium skillet for 10 minutes. Remove from the heat to cool. Whisk the eggs in a large bowl until frothy. Whisk in the cream, Parmesan cheese, shredded cheese, hot sauce, salad dressing mix and spinach. Stir in the sautéed onion. Pour into the baked pie shell. Bake at 350 degrees for 35 to 40 minutes or until the top is brown and a knife inserted in the center comes out clean. **Serves 8.**

Contributed by Allison Beasley

You can grow old and ugly, but if you are a good cook the world will still beat a path to your door. —James Beard

Spring Vegetable Quiche

4 eggs
1¹/2 cups milk
1 cup (4 ounces) shredded
    Cheddar cheese

1 (10-ounce) package frozen chopped
    spinach, thawed and squeezed dry
1 envelope spring vegetable soup mix
1 frozen (9-inch) deep-dish pie shell

Beat the eggs lightly in a large bowl. Add the milk, cheese, spinach and soup mix and mix well. Pour into the frozen pie shell and place on a baking sheet. Bake at 350 degrees for 50 minutes or until a knife inserted in the center comes out clean. **Serves 6.**

Contributed by Anne Brown

Breakfast Bacon Cheese Soufflé

10 slices white bread
6 eggs
3 cups milk
3 tablespoons parsley
1 teaspoon dry mustard

¹/2 teaspoon salt
2 cups chopped cooked bacon, ham,
    sausage or canned shrimp
2 cups (8 ounces) shredded cheese

Trim the crusts from the bread. Cut the bread into cubes. Beat the eggs, milk, parsley, dry mustard and salt in a large bowl until blended. Stir in the bread cubes, bacon and cheese. Pour into a 7×11-inch baking pan. Bake at 325 degrees for 55 to 60 minutes or until set. **Serves 8.**

Contributed by Arlene Moore

Pizza Sauce Omelet

2 eggs, beaten
Pizza sauce

Shredded mozzarella cheese
Sliced pepperoni

Pour the eggs into a skillet coated with nonstick cooking spray, tilting the skillet for even coverage. Cook over medium heat until the eggs set, lifting the edge of the omelet gently with a spatula as the eggs set to allow the uncooked eggs to flow underneath; do not stir. Slide onto a microwave-safe plate. Spread pizza sauce onto one-half of the omelet and sprinkle with cheese and pepperoni. Fold over the remaining half of the omelet to cover the toppings. Microwave on High until the cheese melts and the sauce is heated through. Additional suggestions for toppings include cooked Italian sausage, chopped onion, chopped green bell pepper and sliced black olives. **Serves 1.**

My father made these omelets for us when we were children, and we still look forward to them as adults.

Contributed by Sarah Winkel

Egg and Sausage Pie

12 ounces bulk pork sausage
4 eggs, lightly beaten
3/4 cup milk
1/4 teaspoon basil
1/4 teaspoon salt
1/8 teaspoon pepper

1 (8-count) can refrigerator
    crescent rolls
1 cup (4 ounces) shredded
    Cheddar cheese
1 cup (4 ounces) shredded Monterey
    Jack cheese

Brown the sausage in a skillet, stirring until crumbly; drain. Beat the eggs, milk, basil, salt and pepper in a bowl. Unroll the crescent roll dough in a greased 9×9-inch baking pan, pressing to seal the perforations. Layer the sausage, Cheddar cheese and Monterey Jack cheese over the dough. Pour the egg mixture over the top. Bake at 350 degrees for 23 to 30 minutes or until set. Let stand for 5 minutes before serving. **Serves 9.**

Contributed by Lisa Joubert

Sausage Tartlets

12 ounces 50% less fat bulk
    pork sausage
1¼ cups (5 ounces) shredded
    Monterey Jack cheese
1¼ cups (5 ounces) shredded sharp
    Cheddar cheese

Dash of cayenne pepper
1 cup ranch salad dressing
1 (4-ounce) can chopped black olives
3 (15-count) packages miniature
    phyllo shells

Brown the sausage in a skillet, stirring until finely crumbled. Drain the sausage and wipe the skillet clean. Return the sausage to the skillet. Add the Monterey Jack cheese, Cheddar cheese, cayenne pepper, salad dressing and olives. Cook until the cheese is melted and the mixture is thoroughly incorporated, stirring constantly. Spoon the mixture by teaspoonfuls into the phyllo shells. Place the filled phyllo shells on a baking sheet and bake at 350 degrees for 8 to 10 minutes or until light brown. Serve immediately. **Makes 45.**

Contributed by Anne Brown

Breakfast Before

1 pound bulk pork sausage
6 eggs
2 cups milk
1 teaspoon salt

1 teaspoon dry mustard
2 slices white bread, cut into cubes
1 cup (4 ounces) shredded
    Cheddar cheese

Brown the sausage in a skillet, stirring until crumbly; drain. Beat the eggs, milk, salt and dry mustard in a bowl. Layer the bread, sausage and cheese in a 9×13-inch baking dish. Pour the egg mixture over the top. Chill, covered, for 3 to 10 hours. Uncover and bake at 350 degrees for 45 minutes or until set. **Serves 8.**

Contributed by Jen Yohnka

Morning Sausage Pecan Casserole

1 (8-ounce) package sausage patties
1 (16-ounce) loaf cinnamon-raisin
   bread, cut into cubes
6 eggs
1 1/2 cups milk
1 cup half-and-half
1 teaspoon vanilla extract

1/4 teaspoon nutmeg
1/2 teaspoon cinnamon
1 cup packed brown sugar
1 cup pecans, chopped
1/2 cup (1 stick) butter, softened
2 tablespoons maple syrup

Cook the sausage in a skillet over medium heat until brown on both sides and cooked through. Drain the sausage and cut into bite-size pieces. Layer the bread cubes and sausage in a 9×13-inch baking dish coated with nonstick cooking spray. Beat the eggs, milk, half-and-half, vanilla, nutmeg and cinnamon in a large mixing bowl until blended. Pour over the layers. Chill, covered, for 8 to 10 hours. Mix the brown sugar, pecans, butter and maple syrup in a bowl and mix well. Uncover the baking dish and drop the pecan mixture by teaspoonfuls over the top. Bake at 350 degrees for 35 to 40 minutes or until set. **Serves 6 to 8.**

Contributed by Anne Brown

Breakfast Sausage Bake

1 pound bulk pork sausage, crumbled
6 eggs
2 cups milk
1 teaspoon dry mustard

Salt and pepper to taste
8 ounces Cheddar cheese, shredded
6 slices bread, toasted and crumbled
1 (4-ounce) can chopped green chiles

Brown the sausage in a skillet, stirring until crumbly; drain. Beat the eggs, milk, dry mustard, salt and pepper in a large bowl. Add the cheese, bread, sausage and green chiles and mix well. Spoon into a greased 9×13-inch baking dish. Bake at 350 degrees for 40 minutes. **Serves 8 to 10.**

Contributed by Sandy Malposuto

Mexican "Fudge"

6 eggs
1 (16-ounce) jar taco sauce
4 cups (16 ounces) shredded Cheddar cheese
4 cups (16 ounces) shredded mozzarella cheese

Beat the eggs and taco sauce in a small bowl until blended. Mix the Cheddar cheese and mozzarella cheese together in a bowl. Layer the cheese mixture and taco sauce mixture one-half at a time in a 9×13-inch baking dish, ending with the taco sauce mixture. Bake at 350 degrees for 10 to 15 minutes or until the cheese is melted and bubbly. **Serves 8 to 12.**

Contributed by Sarah Winkel

Slow-Cooker Oatmeal

6 cups water
3 cups rolled oats
Dash of salt

Combine the water, oats and salt in a slow cooker and stir to mix well. Cook on Low for 3 hours or longer. This recipe can easily be doubled. **Serves 4.**

Contributed by Sherri Crawford

Granola

6 cups rolled oats
2 cups shredded coconut
2 cups sliced almonds
1/3 cup vegetable oil
1/2 cup (1 stick) butter
1/2 cup honey
2/3 cup packed brown sugar
1/3 cup granulated sugar
1 teaspoon cinnamon
1/2 teaspoon salt
4 teaspoons vanilla extract
1/2 cup raisins or other dried fruit

Mix the oats, coconut and almonds in a large bowl. Combine the oil, butter, honey, brown sugar, granulated sugar, cinnamon and salt in a saucepan. Simmer over medium heat for 5 minutes, stirring frequently. Remove from the heat and stir in the vanilla. Pour over the oat mixture and mix well to coat. Spread on a baking sheet. Bake at 300 degrees for 30 minutes, turning every 10 minutes with a spatula. Remove from the oven and stir in the raisins. Cool for 1 hour or longer. Store in an airtight container. **Serves 9.**

Contributed by Kerri Lilienthal

Puffed Apple Pancake

1 cup milk
4 eggs
2/3 cup all-purpose flour
3 tablespoons granulated sugar
1 teaspoon vanilla extract
1/2 teaspoon salt
1/4 teaspoon cinnamon
1/4 cup (1/2 stick) unsalted butter
12 ounces Golden Delicious apples,
    peeled, cored and thinly sliced (about 2)
3 tablespoons brown sugar
Confectioners' sugar

Whisk the milk, eggs, flour, granulated sugar, vanilla, salt and cinnamon in a bowl until the batter is smooth. Place the butter in a 9×13-inch glass baking dish and bake at 425 degrees for 5 minutes or until melted. Remove from the oven and cover the bottom of the baking dish with the apples. Bake for 10 minutes or until the apples begin to soften and the butter is bubbly. Pour the batter over the apples and sprinkle with the brown sugar. Bake for 20 minutes or until puffed and brown. Sprinkle with confectioners' sugar. Serve warm with syrup, if desired. **Serves 4.**

Contributed by Leslie Geoffrey

If you can't stand the heat, get out of the kitchen. —Harry S. Truman

Christopher's Famous Pancakes

2 eggs
1 1/2 cups milk
1/3 cup vegetable oil
1 cup all-purpose flour

1 cup whole wheat flour
2 tablespoons brown sugar
2 tablespoons baking powder
1/4 teaspoon salt

Beat the eggs with a hand mixer in a medium mixing bowl until fluffy. Add the milk, oil, all-purpose flour, whole wheat flour, brown sugar, baking powder and salt and beat well until smooth. Pour 1/4 cup at a time onto a hot lightly greased griddle. Cook until golden brown on both sides, turning once. **Makes 15 pancakes.**

Contributed by Krista Borschnack

Overnight Butterscotch Rolls

12 to 15 frozen dinner roll dough balls
1/2 (4-ounce) package butterscotch
    cook-and-serve pudding mix
6 tablespoons butter

1/2 cup packed brown sugar
2 tablespoons light corn syrup
1/2 teaspoon cinnamon

Place the frozen dough balls in a bundt pan and sprinkle with the pudding mix. Melt the butter in a small saucepan. Stir in the brown sugar, corn syrup and cinnamon. Heat until the brown sugar is dissolved, stirring constantly. Pour over the dough. Cover and let rise at room temperature for 8 to 10 hours. Bake at 325 degrees for 25 to 30 minutes or until golden brown. **Serves 4 to 6.**

Contributed by Christine Betts

Williamsburg Bread

2 (8-count) cans refrigerator
   crescent rolls
16 ounces cream cheese, softened
1 egg yolk

1 cup granulated sugar
1 teaspoon vanilla extract
1 egg white, lightly beaten
Cinnamon-sugar to taste

Unroll one can of the crescent roll dough into a buttered 9×13-inch baking dish, pressing to seal the perforations. Beat the cream cheese, egg yolk, granulated sugar and vanilla in a mixing bowl until smooth. Spread evenly over the dough. Unroll the remaining can of crescent roll dough and place over the top, pressing to seal the perforations. Brush with the egg white and sprinkle with cinnamon-sugar. Bake at 350 degrees for 25 minutes. **Serves 8 to 10.**

Contributed by Christine Betts

Book Club Banana Nut Bread

^{1}/2 cup vegetable oil
 1^1/4 cups sugar
 2 eggs
 5 ripe bananas
 2 cups all-purpose flour

1 teaspoon baking soda
1 teaspoon salt
2 tablespoons honey wheat germ
1 cup walnuts or pecans, chopped

Beat the oil and sugar in a mixing bowl. Add the eggs and bananas and beat until the bananas are thoroughly mashed. Sift the flour, baking soda and salt in a bowl. Stir in the wheat germ and walnuts. Add to the banana mixture and mix just until incorporated. Pour evenly into two greased 5×8-inch loaf pans. Bake at 350 degrees for 50 minutes or until the tops spring back when pressed. **Makes 2 loaves.**

I often make this bread for my book club friends.

Contributed by Allison Beasley

Banana Nut Bread with Cream Cheese Frosting

BREAD
2 teaspoons baking soda
1 tablespoon warm water
2 teaspoons vinegar
1/2 cup milk
4 egg yolks
3 cups sugar
1 cup (2 sticks) butter, softened
3 cups all-purpose flour
2 teaspoons vanilla extract
2 cups mashed bananas
   (about 5 bananas)

1 cup chopped nuts
4 egg whites, stiffly beaten

CREAM CHEESE FROSTING
8 ounces cream cheese, softened
1/2 cup (1 stick) butter, softened
1 (1-pound) package confectioners'
   sugar
1 teaspoon vanilla extract

To prepare the bread, dissolve the baking soda in the water in a cup and set aside. Stir the vinegar into the milk and set aside. Beat the egg yolks, sugar and butter in a mixing bowl until well mixed. Add the milk mixture and flour alternately, beating until incorporated after each addition. Add the baking soda mixture and vanilla and mix until well blended. Stir in the bananas and nuts. Fold in the egg whites. Pour into three greased 5×8-inch loaf pans. Bake at 350 degrees for 45 to 60 minutes or until the loaves test done. Invert onto a wire rack to cool.

To prepare the frosting, beat the cream cheese and butter in a mixing bowl until light and fluffy. Add the confectioners' sugar and vanilla and beat until smooth. Spread over the cool loaves. Store in the refrigerator. **Makes 3 loaves.**

For Banana Nut Cake, bake the batter in two 8-inch cake pans. Spread apricot or strawberry preserves between the cooled cake layers before frosting the top and side.

Contributed by Bernadette Henriott

Banana Nut Bread

1/2 cup shortening	2 cups all-purpose flour
1 1/2 cups sugar	1/2 teaspoon baking soda
2 eggs	1 teaspoon salt
1 1/2 cups milk	1 1/2 cups mashed bananas (about 3
1 teaspoon vanilla extract	medium)
1 teaspoon vinegar	1 cup chopped nuts

Beat the shortening, sugar and eggs in a mixing bowl until smooth. Add the milk, vanilla and vinegar and mix well. Beat in the flour, baking soda and salt until smooth. Stir in the bananas and nuts. Pour into two greased 5×8-inch loaf pans. Bake at 350 degrees for 1 hour and 20 minutes. **Makes 2 loaves.**

Contributed by Former First Lady LuraLynn Ryan

Easy Banana Nut Bread

2 cups sifted all-purpose flour	1 cup sugar
1 teaspoon baking soda	2 eggs, beaten
1 teaspoon salt	3 bananas, mashed
1/2 cup (1 stick) butter or	1/2 cup nuts, chopped
margarine, melted	

Sift the sifted flour, baking soda and salt together. Combine the butter and sugar in a bowl and stir to mix well. Beat in the eggs. Add the flour mixture and mix well. Stir in the bananas and nuts. Pour into a greased 5×8-inch loaf pan. Bake at 350 degrees for 1 hour. **Serves 8.**

Contributed by Katie Reed

Banana Bread

1/2 cup (1 stick) margarine, melted   1 teaspoon baking soda
1 cup sugar   1 teaspoon salt
2 eggs   2 bananas, mashed
2 cups all-purpose flour

Combine the margarine and sugar in a mixing bowl and mix well. Beat in the eggs. Add the flour, baking soda, salt and bananas and beat well. Pour into a greased 5×8-inch loaf pan. Bake at 350 degrees for 1 hour. **Serves 6.**

Contributed by Tiffany Holohan

Strawberry Bread

3 cups all-purpose flour   4 eggs, beaten
2 cups sugar   3/4 cup vegetable oil
1 teaspoon baking soda   2 1/2 cups fresh or frozen strawberries,
1 teaspoon salt   mashed
1 teaspoon cinnamon

Mix the flour, sugar, baking soda, salt and cinnamon in a large bowl. Add the eggs and oil and mix well. Stir in the strawberries. Pour into two greased 4×8-inch loaf pans. Bake at 350 degrees for 1 hour or until the loaves test done. **Makes 2 loaves.**

This bread freezes well.

Contributed by Anne Brown

Poppy Seed Bread

BREAD
4 eggs
3^{1}/$_{4}$ cups sugar
2^{1}/$_{4}$ cups milk
1^{1}/$_{2}$ cups vegetable oil
3/4 teaspoon vanilla extract
3/4 teaspoon butter flavoring
4^{1}/$_{2}$ cups all-purpose flour
2^{1}/$_{4}$ teaspoons baking powder
1 teaspoon salt
2^{1}/$_{4}$ teaspoons poppy seeds

ORANGE GLAZE
1 cup sugar
^{1}/$_{3}$ cup orange juice
3/4 teaspoon almond extract
3/4 teaspoon butter flavoring
3/4 teaspoon vanilla extract

To prepare the bread, combine the eggs, sugar, milk, oil, vanilla and butter flavoring in a mixing bowl and beat well. Add the flour, baking powder and salt and beat until smooth. Stir in the poppy seeds. Pour into three greased and floured 5×8-inch loaf pans. Bake at 325 degrees for 1 hour. Remove to wire racks to cool.

To prepare the glaze, beat the sugar, orange juice, almond extract, butter flavoring and vanilla in a bowl until smooth. Spoon over the cooled loaves. **Makes 3 loaves.**

Contributed by Bernadette Henriott

Irish Soda Bread

4 cups all-purpose flour
1 tablespoon sugar
2 teaspoons cream of tartar
1 teaspoon baking soda
1/2 teaspoon salt
1 1/2 cups raisins
1 egg, beaten
1 1/2 cups buttermilk

Sift the flour, sugar, cream of tartar, baking soda and salt into a large bowl. Add the raisins and stir to coat. Stir in the egg and buttermilk. Place the dough on a lightly floured surface and knead thoroughly. Shape the dough into a ball with a flat bottom and place on a buttered baking sheet. Make the sign of the cross with a sharp knife on top of the loaf. Bake at 350 degrees for 45 to 60 minutes or until golden brown. **Serves 8.**

This family recipe originated in Ireland and has been handed down over the years.

Contributed by Ann O' Gorman

Easy Dinner Rolls

2 envelopes dry yeast
1 cup warm water (105 to 115 degrees)
1/2 cup (1 stick) butter, melted
1/2 cup sugar
3 eggs
1 teaspoon salt
4 to 41/2 cups unbleached all-purpose flour
Melted butter (optional)

Dissolve the yeast in the water in a large bowl. Let stand for 5 minutes or until foamy. Stir in 1/2 cup butter, the sugar, eggs and salt. Beat in the flour 1 cup at a time until the dough is too stiff to mix. (You may not need all of the flour.) Cover and chill for 8 hours or up to 4 days. Place the chilled dough on a lightly floured surface. Divide the dough into two equal portions. Roll each portion into a smooth ball and place in a greased 9×13-inch baking pan. Cover and let rise for 1 hour or until doubled in bulk. Bake at 375 degrees for 15 to 20 minutes or until the rolls are golden brown. Brush with melted butter. Break apart to serve. **Serves 24.**

Contributed by Lesley Robinson

Appetizers and Beverages

Momence Island Bridge

Clock Tower at
Shapiro Developmental Center

Summertime Bruschetta

10 Roma tomatoes, chopped
1 (7-ounce) jar sun-dried tomatoes
1 small red onion, chopped
1/4 cup olive oil

3 tablespoons lemon juice
4 large basil leaves, sliced
Salt and pepper to taste
1 sourdough baguette, baked

Combine the Roma tomatoes, sun-dried tomatoes and onion in a bowl and mix well. Stir in the olive oil and lemon juice. Season with the basil, salt and pepper. Cut the bread into slices 1/4 inch thick and spread each slice with the tomato mixture. You may use small garlic toasts instead of the baguette. **Serves 8.**

Contributed by Arlene Moore

Crawford's Hillbilly Bruschetta

2 cups (8 ounces) shredded
    Cheddar cheese
3/4 cup mayonnaise

1/3 cup crumbled bacon
1 loaf French bread

Mix the cheese, mayonnaise and bacon in a bowl. Cut the bread into slices 1/2 inch thick. Spread the cheese mixture on each bread slice and place on a baking sheet. Bake at 425 degrees for 8 to 10 minutes or until golden brown and bubbly. **Serves 6.**

Contributed by Sherri Crawford

Cheese and Pesto Toasts

1/2 cup pesto
1 loaf Italian bread, sliced
5 plum tomatoes, sliced
8 ounces sharp Cheddar cheese, sliced

Spread the pesto on each slice of the bread. Top each with a tomato slice and cheese slice and place on a baking sheet. Broil for 2 to 3 minutes or until the cheese melts. **Serves 8.**

Contributed by Sherri Crawford

Mediterranean Marinated Cheese

8 ounces cream cheese
1/2 cup sun-dried tomato vinaigrette
1 teaspoon black peppercorns
2 garlic cloves, sliced
Peel of 1 lemon, cut into thin strips
6 sprigs of fresh thyme, cut into pieces
3 small sprigs of rosemary, stems removed

Cut the cream cheese into thirty-six cubes and place in a 9-inch pie plate. Add the vinaigrette, peppercorns, garlic, lemon peel strips, thyme and rosemary and toss to coat. Marinate, covered, in the refrigerator for 1 to 24 hours. Serve with crackers, crusty bread or pita chips. **Serves 8.**

Contributed by Lesley Robinson

It's difficult to think anything but pleasant thoughts while eating a homegrown tomato.
—Louis Grizzard

Cherry-Sauced Meatballs

MEATBALLS

2 cups loosely-packed torn
    white bread
1/2 cup milk
1 teaspoon soy sauce
1 teaspoon garlic salt
1/4 teaspoon onion powder
8 ounces ground beef
8 ounces hot bulk pork sausage
1 (8-ounce) can sliced water chestnuts,
    drained and chopped

CHERRY SAUCE

1 (21-ounce) can cherry pie filling
1/3 cup dry sherry
1/4 cup white vinegar
1/4 cup steak sauce
2 tablespoons brown sugar
2 tablespoons soy sauce

To prepare the meatballs, combine the bread, milk, soy sauce, garlic salt and onion powder in a bowl and stir to mix well. Mix the ground beef and sausage together in a bowl. Add to the bread mixture and mix well. Add the water chestnuts and mix well. Shape into 3/4-inch balls and place on a lightly greased rack in a broiler pan. Bake at 350 degrees for 20 minutes.

To prepare the sauce and assemble, combine the pie filling, sherry, vinegar, steak sauce, brown sugar and soy sauce in a saucepan and mix well. Cook over medium heat until heated through, stirring constantly. Place the meatballs in a chafing dish. Pour the sauce over the meatballs and stir to coat. **Serves 8.**

Contributed by Lesley Robinson

Crawford's Famous Enchilada Meatballs

1 (10-ounce) can cream of
   mushroom soup
1 (10-ounce) can tomato soup
1 (10-ounce) can enchilada sauce
2 cups (8 ounces) shredded Cheddar
   cheese, or more to taste

Chili powder to taste
Crushed red pepper to taste
1/2 to 3/4 (6-pound) package
   frozen meatballs

Cook the mushroom soup, tomato soup and enchilada sauce in a large saucepan over medium heat until heated through. Add the cheese and cook until melted, stirring constantly. Stir in the chili powder and crushed red pepper. Microwave the meatballs in a microwave-safe dish on High until cooked through; drain. Add to the sauce and stir to coat. Place in a slow cooker and heat on Low until ready to serve. **Serves 10.**

Contributed by Sherri Crawford

Andria's Crab-Stuffed Mushrooms

1 pound medium-large mushrooms
12 ounces cream cheese, softened
1/4 cup mayonnaise
1/4 cup sour cream
1/2 teaspoon dill weed
1/2 teaspoon Italian seasoning

1/2 teaspoon seasoned salt
1/2 teaspoon garlic
1/4 cup (1 ounce) grated
   Parmesan cheese
12 ounces crab meat or imitation
   crab meat

Clean the mushrooms and remove the stems. Combine the cream cheese, mayonnaise, sour cream, dill weed, Italian seasoning, seasoned salt, garlic and Parmesan cheese in a bowl and mix well. Stir in the crab meat. Place a heaping spoonful of the filling in each mushroom cap and place on a greased baking sheet. Bake at 400 degrees for 20 to 25 minutes or until heated through. **Serves 6 to 8.**

Contributed by Gail Passwater

Water Chestnut Wraps

1 pound sliced bacon
2 (6-ounce) cans whole water
    chestnuts, drained
12 ounces ketchup
1/2 cup granulated sugar

1/2 cup packed brown sugar
Juice of 1 lemon
2 tablespoons Worcestershire sauce
2 tablespoons molasses

Cut the bacon slices into halves. Wrap a bacon half around each water chestnut and secure with a wooden pick. Place on a rack in a broiler pan and broil for 5 minutes. Turn and broil for 5 minutes longer or until the bacon is crisp. Combine the ketchup, granulated sugar, brown sugar, lemon juice, Worcestershire sauce and molasses in a bowl and mix well. Pour into a serving dish. Serve with the water chestnuts. **Makes 2 dozen.**

Contributed by Anne Brown

Ranch Pinwheels

16 ounces cream cheese, softened
1 envelope ranch salad dressing mix
2 green onions, chopped
4 (12-inch) flour tortillas

1 (4-ounce) jar diced pimentos
1 (4-ounce) can chopped green chiles
1 (2-ounce) can sliced black olives

Combine the cream cheese, salad dressing mix and green onions in a bowl and mix well. Spread on one side of each tortilla. Drain the pimentos, green chiles and olives and pat dry. Sprinkle equal amounts of the pimentos, green chiles and olives over the cream cheese layer and roll up the tortillas tightly. Chill, covered, for at least 2 hours. Uncover and cut each roll-up into 1-inch slices, discarding the ends. Arrange spiral-side up on a serving tray. **Makes 3 dozen.**

Contributed by Tiffany Holohan

Vegetable Cheese Wraps

16 ounces Neufchâtel cheese or cream cheese, softened
2 green onions, finely chopped
1 envelope ranch salad dressing mix
1 (10-count) package spinach tortillas or plain flour tortillas
1/2 red bell pepper, finely chopped

1 small green bell pepper, finely chopped
1 (2-ounce) can sliced black olives, drained and chopped
2 cups (8 ounces) finely shredded Colby Jack cheese

Process the Neufchâtel cheese, green onions and salad dressing mix in a food processor until blended. Spread a thin layer on each tortilla. Sprinkle each with the bell peppers, olives and Colby Jack cheese. Roll up tightly and chill, covered, for 3 hours. Unwrap and cut into 1 1/2-inch slices and secure with wooden picks. Serve on a bed of lettuce. You may add 1/3 pound thinly sliced turkey. **Serves 12 to 16.**

Contributed by Katie Reed

Freezer Ham Sandwiches

1/2 cup (1 stick) margarine, softened
2 tablespoons poppy seeds
1/4 cup chopped chives

1/4 cup mustard
12 soft Kaiser rolls
24 slices Swiss cheese
2 to 3 pounds deli ham, thinly sliced

Combine the margarine, poppy seeds, chives and mustard in a bowl and mix well. Split the rolls into halves and spread each side with the mustard mixture. Layer one-half of the cheese, the ham and remaining cheese on the bottom halves of the rolls. Replace the top halves of the rolls and wrap in foil. Freeze until ready to serve. To serve, bake in the foil at 375 degrees for 45 minutes if frozen or for 25 minutes if thawed. **Makes 12 sandwiches.**

These are great to keep in the freezer in case company stops by.

Contributed by Lisa Hammes

Green Olive and Walnut Spread

1/3 cup canola oil
3 tablespoons lemon juice
1 cup stuffed green olives
1 cup walnut pieces

1/2 cup chopped fresh parsley
1/2 cup chopped green onions
1/2 teaspoon crushed red pepper flakes
Salt and black pepper to taste

Process the canola oil, lemon juice, green olives, walnut pieces, parsley, green onions and red pepper flakes in a food processor just until the mixture holds together. Do not overprocess. The mixture should have a coarse texture. Season with salt and black pepper. Spoon into a serving bowl. Chill, covered, in the refrigerator. Serve with assorted crackers. **Serves 8.**

Contributed by Missie Rolinitis

Crab Fondue

8 ounces canned crab meat
3/4 cup mayonnaise
1 onion, chopped
1 cup (4 ounces) grated asiago cheese
Paprika
1 loaf French or sourdough bread, cut into cubes

Combine the crab meat, mayonnaise, onion, cheese and paprika in a saucepan. Heat until the cheese melts, stirring constantly. Spoon into a fondue pot. Serve with the bread cubes. **Serves 8.**

Contributed by Sherri Crawford

Parmesan Fondue

16 ounces cream cheese, softened
1¹/2 to 2 cups milk
¹/2 teaspoon garlic salt

1¹/2 cups (6 ounces) grated
    Parmesan cheese
1 loaf French bread, cut into cubes

Combine the cream cheese and milk in a saucepan. Cook over low heat until the cream cheese melts, stirring constantly. Stir in the garlic salt and Parmesan cheese. Cook until heated through, stirring constantly. Spoon into a fondue pot. Serve with the bread cubes. **Serves 8.**

Contributed by Sherri Crawford

Pastry-Wrapped Brie Cheese with Raspberry Filling

¹/2 cup raspberry preserves
¹/4 cup fresh or frozen
    raspberries, thawed

1 sheet frozen puff pastry
1 (13-ounce) wheel baby Brie cheese
1 egg, beaten

Combine the preserves and raspberries in a small bowl and mix well. Roll the pastry into a 12-inch square on a lightly floured surface. Cut the top rind off of the cheese. Place the cheese cut side up in the center of the pastry. Spoon the raspberry mixture over the top of the cheese. Fold the pastry on two opposite sides over the cheese. Brush the two remaining sides with some of the beaten egg and fold over the cheese, pressing the seams to seal. Brush the top of the pastry with the remaining beaten egg and place on a baking sheet. Bake at 400 degrees for 30 minutes or until the pastry is a deep golden brown. The pastry may split. Remove from the oven and let cool for 15 minutes. Place on a serving platter and serve with assorted crackers or baguette slices. **Serves 6 to 8.**

Contributed by Leslie Geoffrey

Brie Cheese with Cranberry Relish

¹/₂ cup sugar
¹/₂ cup water
¹/₂ (12-ounce) package fresh
    cranberries
2 scallions, chopped
    (green portion only)
¹/₄ cup fresh cilantro, chopped

Juice of 1 lime
¹/₂ teaspoon lime zest
¹/₂ teaspoon ginger
Dash of salt
1 wheel Brie cheese or
    Camembert cheese

Bring the sugar and water to a boil in a small saucepan. Add the cranberries and return to a boil and cook for 10 minutes. Remove from the heat to cool. Pulse the cool cranberry mixture, scallions, cilantro, lime juice, lime zest, ginger and salt in a food processor until thoroughly incorporated. Pour into a serving dish. Serve on top of the cheese with assorted crackers or crostini. The relish can be made up to 2 days ahead. Store in an airtight container in the refrigerator. **Serves 6 to 8.**

Contributed by Anne Brown

Triple-Berry Salsa

1 cup strawberries, slivered
1 cup blueberries
¹/₂ cup raspberries
1 large or 2 medium Granny Smith
    apples, cored, peeled and chopped

1 kiwifruit, chopped
Juice of 1 small orange
Zest of 1 small orange
2 tablespoons apple cider
1 tablespoon brown sugar

Combine the strawberries, blueberries, raspberries, apples and kiwifruit in a large bowl. Stir in the orange juice, orange zest, apple cider and brown sugar gently. Spoon into a chilled serving dish. **Serves 6 to 8.**

Contributed by Rochelle McAvoy

Fruit Cocktail Cheese Ball

16 ounces cream cheese, softened
1 (4-ounce) package vanilla instant pudding mix
2 tablespoons orange juice
1 (16-ounce) can fruit cocktail, drained
Slivered almonds or shredded coconut

Beat the cream cheese, pudding mix and orange juice in a mixing bowl until smooth. Fold in the fruit cocktail. Shape into a ball and roll in the almonds. Serve with graham crackers. **Serves 6 to 8.**

Contributed by Jen Yohnka

Peach Jalapeño Dip

8 ounces cream cheese, softened
1 green onion bulb, chopped
1/4 cup chopped jalapeño chiles
1/4 cup peach preserves

Combine the cream cheese, onion, jalapeño chiles and preserves in a bowl and mix well. Serve with honey wheat pretzel sticks. **Serves 8.**

Contributed by Sherri Crawford

Artichoke Dip

1 (14-ounce) can artichoke hearts, drained and chopped
1 cup mayonnaise
1 cup (4 ounces) grated Parmesan cheese
Salt and garlic salt to taste
Hot red pepper sauce to taste (optional)

Combine the artichoke hearts, mayonnaise and cheese in a bowl and mix well. Season with salt, garlic salt and hot sauce. Spread in a 9×13-inch baking dish. Bake at 350 degrees for 10 to 15 minutes or until brown and bubbly. Serve with assorted crackers or pita bread. **Serves 12 to 15.**

Contributed by Sarah Winkel

Spinach Dip

1 1/4 cups sour cream
1 cup mayonnaise
1 envelope vegetable soup mix
1 (8-ounce) can water chestnuts, drained and chopped
1 (10-ounce) package frozen chopped spinach,
    thawed and squeezed dry
3 green onions, chopped

Mix the sour cream, mayonnaise and soup mix in a bowl until blended. Stir in the water chestnuts, spinach and green onions. Chill, covered, for 2 hours. Stir again before serving. Serve with Hawaiian bread, assorted chips or vegetables for dipping. **Serves 8 to 10.**

Contributed by Sarah Winkel

Bean Dip

1 (9-ounce) can bean dip
2 cups sour cream
1 envelope taco seasoning mix
2 or 3 green onions, chopped
1 tomato, chopped
Chopped black olives
Finely shredded Cheddar cheese

Spread the bean dip evenly in a 9×13-inch dish. Mix the sour cream and taco seasoning mix in a bowl. Spread over the bean dip. Sprinkle with the green onions, tomato, black olives and cheese. Chill, covered, in the refrigerator. Serve with tortilla chips. **Serves 6 to 8.**

Contributed by Kathy Kinmonth

Buffalo Dip

1 large can chicken, chopped
2/3 cup ranch salad dressing
1/3 cup buffalo wing sauce
8 ounces cream cheese, softened
2 cups (8 ounces) Cheddar cheese

Combine the chicken, salad dressing, buffalo wing sauce, cream cheese and Cheddar cheese in a bowl and mix well. Spread evenly in a shallow baking dish. Bake at 350 degrees for 12 to 15 minutes or until heated through. Serve warm with sliced Milano bread or assorted crackers. **Serves 10 to 12.**

Contributed by Kerri Lilienthal

Baked Pizza Dip

8 ounces cream cheese, softened
1 (14-ounce) jar pizza sauce
1 cup (4 ounces) shredded mozzarella cheese, or to taste
Chopped fresh cilantro or parsley (optional)

Spread the cream cheese in a 9-inch pie plate. Spread the pizza sauce over the cream
cheese. Sprinkle with the mozzarella cheese and cilantro. Bake at 350 degrees for
15 to 20 minutes or until the mozzarella cheese melts. Serve with assorted crackers
or chips. **Serves 6 to 8.**

Contributed by Missie Rolinitis

Spicy Herb Roasted Nuts

1/2 cup maple syrup
3 tablespoons olive oil
1 1/2 teaspoons dried oregano
1 1/2 teaspoons dried sage
1 1/2 teaspoons dried thyme
1 1/2 teaspoons dried rosemary

1 1/2 teaspoons dried marjoram
1/4 teaspoon cayenne pepper
1 1/2 cups whole almonds
1 1/2 cups walnut halves
1 cup pecans
Kosher salt to taste

Combine the maple syrup, olive oil, oregano, sage, thyme, rosemary, marjoram and
cayenne pepper in a bowl and mix well. Let stand at room temperature for 1 hour.
Mix the almonds, walnuts and pecans in a large bowl. Pour the maple syrup mixture
over the nut mixture and stir to coat. Spread on a rimmed baking sheet and sprinkle
with kosher salt. Bake at 300 degrees for 1 hour or until all of the liquid evaporates,
stirring occasionally. Store in an airtight container. **Serves 8 to 10.**

Contributed by Anne Brown

Almond Tea

1 1/2 cups sugar, or 3 tablespoons liquid sweetener
16 cups water
2 tablespoons lemon-flavored instant iced tea mix
1 (6-ounce) can frozen orange juice concentrate, thawed
1 (6-ounce) can frozen lemonade concentrate, thawed
1 teaspoon vanilla extract
1 teaspoon almond extract

Dissolve the sugar in 12 cups of the water in a 1-gallon container. Add the remaining 4 cups water, the iced tea mix, orange juice concentrate, lemonade concentrate, vanilla and almond extract and mix well. Chill in the refrigerator until ready to serve. **Serves 8 to 12.**

A great drink for a little girls' party.

Contributed by Sarah Bowman-Steffes

Jack Frost Cocktail

1 ounce Godiva white chocolate liqueur or crème de cacao
3/4 ounce peppermint schnapps
1 ounce vanilla vodka
Ice

Process the liqueur, schnapps, vodka and a handful of ice in a blender until a frothy consistency. Pour into a serving glass and garnish with a candy cane. Peppermint ice cream may be used instead of the ice. Blend until of the desired consistency. **Serves 1.**

Contributed by Jane Koehler

Key Lime Martini

2 ounces Stoli vanilla vodka
2 ounces sweet-and-sour mix
1 ounce pineapple juice
Ice

Combine the vodka, sweet-and-sour mix and pineapple juice in a cocktail shaker. Add enough ice to fill and shake to mix well. Strain into a martini glass. **Serves 1.**

Contributed by Jane Koehler

Pink Squirrel

1 tablespoon white crème de cacao
1 ounce crème de noyaux
1 tablespoon light cream
1 cup vanilla ice cream

Process the crème de cacao, crème de noyaux, cream and ice cream in a blender until smooth. Pour into cocktail glasses. **Serves 2.**

Contributed by Karen Johnston-Gentry

Never trust a skinny cook. —Author unknown

White Zinfandel Sangria

1 (750-milliliter) bottle white
    zinfandel, chilled
1/2 cup peach schnapps
2 tablespoons orange liqueur
2 tablespoons sugar

2 cinnamon sticks, broken into halves
1 lemon, sliced
1 orange, sliced
1 peach, sliced into wedges
1 (10-ounce) bottle club soda, chilled

Combine the wine, schnapps, orange liqueur, sugar, cinnamon sticks, lemon, orange and peach in a tall pitcher and mix well. Chill for 30 minutes or longer. Stir in the club soda. Fill six wine glasses with ice. Strain the sangria into the glasses and serve. **Serves 6.**

Contributed by Lisa Joubert

Vodka Slush

1 (12-ounce) can frozen lemonade
    concentrate, thawed
1 (12-ounce) can frozen orange juice
    concentrate, thawed
2 cups prepared instant tea

1 (3-ounce) package strawberry
    gelatin, prepared (not chilled or set)
4 cups cold water
2 cups vodka
Lemon-lime soda

Mix the lemonade concentrate, orange juice concentrate, tea, liquid gelatin, cold water and vodka in a large freezer container. Freeze until slushy. To serve, add 1 scoop of the slush to each glass and fill with lemon-lime soda. **Serves 12.**

Contributed by Sherri Crawford

Soups and Salads

Former First Lady **Lura Lynn Ryan** sits on a bench at the
Kankakee County Courthouse. The bench was placed there in honor
of her and her husband, Former Illinois Governor George Ryan, as
thanks from the people of Kankakee County for their years of service
and contributions to area communities. The bench incorporates three
of her favorite things: children, the arts, and reading.

Looking Down The River.
From The Riverview Hotel.

The Kankakee River

Pasta Fagioli

1 pound ground beef
1 small onion, chopped (1 cup)
1 cup sliced carrots
1 cup sliced celery
2 garlic cloves, minced
2 (14-ounce) cans diced tomatoes
1 (15-ounce) can Great
   Northern beans
1 (15-ounce) can red kidney beans
1 (15-ounce) can tomato sauce

1 (12-ounce) can vegetable
   juice cocktail
1 tablespoon white vinegar
1 1/2 teaspoons salt
1 teaspoon oregano
1 teaspoon basil
1/2 teaspoon pepper
1/2 teaspoon thyme
6 to 8 cups water
8 ounces ditali

Brown the ground beef in a large saucepan over medium heat, stirring until crumbly; drain. Add the onion, carrots, celery and garlic and sauté for 10 minutes. Add the tomatoes, undrained beans, tomato sauce, vegetable juice cocktail, vinegar, salt, oregano, basil, pepper and thyme. Simmer for 1 hour.

Bring the water to a boil in a large saucepan. Add the pasta and cook for 10 minutes or until al dente; drain. Add the pasta to the soup and simmer for 5 to 10 minutes or until heated through. Ladle into soup bowls. **Serves 8.**

Contributed by Mary Burgner

Volunteers are not paid—not because they are worthless, but because they are priceless.
—Author unknown

Stuffed Bell Pepper Soup

1 pound ground beef
8 cups water
4 cups tomato juice
3 red or green bell peppers
1 1/2 cups chili sauce
1 cup long grain rice
2 ribs celery, chopped
1 large onion, chopped
2 teaspoons browning sauce (optional)
3 chicken bouillon cubes
2 garlic cloves, minced
1/2 teaspoon salt

Brown the ground beef in a large Dutch oven or kettle over medium heat, stirring until crumbly; drain. Add the water, tomato juice, bell peppers, chili sauce, rice, celery, onion, browning sauce, bouillon cubes, garlic and salt. Bring to a boil and reduce the heat. Simmer, uncovered, for 1 hour or until the rice is tender. Ladle into soup bowls. **Serves 16.**

Contributed by Vickie Shreffler

Tis an ill cook that cannot lick his own fingers. —William Shakespeare (Romeo and Juliet)

Meatball Tortellini Soup

8 ounces ground beef
1 small onion, chopped
2 slices bread
3/4 cup (3 ounces) shredded Parmesan cheese
2 large cans chicken broth
1 1/2 cups chopped onions
1 1/2 cups chopped carrots
1 teaspoon basil
1/4 teaspoon hot pepper flakes
2 cups fresh tortellini
1 small zucchini, sliced
3 to 5 ounces spinach, chopped
Freshly grated Parmesan cheese

Process the ground beef, 1 onion, the bread and shredded Parmesan cheese in a food processor until combined. Shape into meatballs and set aside.

Bring the broth, onions, carrots, basil and hot pepper flakes to a boil in a large stockpot. Add the meatballs and simmer for 15 to 20 minutes or until cooked through. Add the pasta and cook until al dente. Stir in the zucchini and spinach. Cook for 3 minutes. Ladle into soup bowls and sprinkle with freshly grated Parmesan cheese. **Serves 6 to 8.**

For meatballs, add 2 to 3 tablespoons milk and salt and pepper to taste while processing.

Contributed by Karen Johnston-Gentry

Sue's Taco Soup

1 pound ground beef
1 envelope ranch salad dressing mix
1 (15-ounce) can black beans, drained
1 (15-ounce) can corn, drained

2 (14-ounce) cans diced tomatoes
1 (14-ounce) can diced tomatoes
   with green chiles

Brown the ground beef in a large saucepan, stirring until crumbly; drain. Stir in the salad dressing mix. Add the black beans, corn, tomatoes and tomatoes with green chiles. Bring to a boil and reduce the heat. Simmer for 30 minutes. Ladle into soup bowls. **Serves 6.**

Contributed by Jen Yohnka

Creamy Ham and Vegetable Soup

3 cups water
1 cup chopped cooked ham
4 potatoes, chopped
1 cup chopped celery
1 cup chopped carrots
1/2 cup chopped onion
2 teaspoons salt

1/4 teaspoon pepper
1/2 cup (1 stick) butter
1/2 cup all-purpose flour
4 cups milk
4 cups (16 ounces) shredded sharp
   Cheddar cheese

Bring the water to a boil in a saucepan. Add the ham, potatoes, celery, carrots, onion, salt and pepper. Cover and simmer for 10 minutes. Melt the butter in a large saucepan. Stir in the flour. Add the milk gradually, stirring constantly. Cook over medium heat until the mixture begins to boil, stirring constantly. Add the cheese. Cook until the cheese melts, stirring constantly. Stir in the ham mixture. Ladle into soup bowls. **Serves 12.**

Anonymous

Chicken Noodle Soup

12 cups chicken broth (2 large cans)
2 cups cubed cooked chicken
1/3 cup chopped onion
1 cup sliced carrots (2 medium)
1 cup sliced celery (3 medium)

1 teaspoon dried parsley
1 small bay leaf
1/2 teaspoon salt
1/4 teaspoon pepper
12 ounces frozen egg noodles

Combine the broth, chicken, onion, carrots, celery, parsley, bay leaf, salt and pepper in a large saucepan and mix well. Bring to a boil and stir in the noodles. Reduce the heat and simmer for 30 minutes or until the noodles are tender, stirring occasionally. Discard the bay leaf. Ladle into soup bowls. **Serves 10 to 12.**

Contributed by Melissa Fischer

Chicken Tortilla Soup

4 chicken breasts, cooked and
    shredded
2 (15-ounce) cans corn
1 (14-ounce) can whole tomatoes
2 (15-ounce) cans kidney beans
3 or 4 garlic cloves, minced

1 (4-ounce) can chopped green chiles
1 teaspoon cumin
1 teaspoon salt
1 teaspoon pepper
3 (14-ounce) cans chicken broth
1/2 cup chopped onion

Combine the chicken, corn, tomatoes and kidney beans in a slow cooker. Add the garlic, undrained green chiles, cumin, salt, pepper, broth and onions and mix well. Cook on High until heated through. Ladle into soup bowls. Serve with shredded cheese, sour cream and crushed tortilla chips. You may chop the tomatoes, if desired. **Serves 8.**

Contributed by Lisa Kick

Chicken Corn Chowder

3 boneless skinless chicken breasts
3 tablespoons all-purpose flour
5 tablespoons butter
1^{1}/$_{2}$ cups heavy whipping cream
1 tablespoon parsley
1 tablespoon cumin
1 teaspoon salt
1 teaspoon pepper
3 cups water
^{1}/$_{2}$ cup chopped white onion
1^{1}/$_{2}$ cups frozen corn kernels
1^{1}/$_{2}$ cups (6 ounces) shredded sharp Cheddar cheese

Boil the chicken in water to cover in a saucepan until tender and cooked through; drain and cool. Chop the chicken and set aside. Brown the flour 1 tablespoon at a time in the butter in a large saucepan. Do not burn. Add the cream gradually, stirring constantly. Remove from the heat. Add the parsley, cumin, salt and pepper and mix well. Stir in the water and return to medium heat. Add the chicken, onion and corn. Cook for 10 to 15 minutes or until heated through. Add the cheese and simmer over low heat for 20 minutes. Ladle into soup bowls. You can add more water if needed. Carrots may also be added to add color. **Serves 4 to 6.**

Contributed by Rochelle McAvoy

Potato, Cheddar Corn Chowder

3 tablespoons butter
1 onion, chopped
1 red bell pepper, chopped
1 tablespoon all-purpose flour
4 cups (32 ounces) vegetable broth
2¹/2 cups chopped Yukon Gold potatoes (about 4 large)
2 cups frozen super sweet corn
2/3 cup milk
1¹/2 cups (6 ounces) shredded sharp Cheddar cheese
Sea salt and freshly ground black pepper to taste
Pinch of cayenne pepper

Melt the butter in a large saucepan over medium-high heat. Add the onion and bell pepper and sauté for 5 minutes or until tender. Stir in the flour to coat. Add the broth and bring to a boil, whisking constantly until smooth. Reduce the heat. Add the potatoes and simmer for 20 minutes or until tender. Mash the potatoes slightly in the soup. Stir in the corn and milk. Cook for 5 minutes and remove from the heat. Stir in the cheese, salt, black pepper and cayenne pepper. Ladle into soup bowls and garnish with chopped parsley. **Serves 6 to 8.**

Contributed by Jane Koehler

A messy kitchen is a happy kitchen and this kitchen is delirious. —Author unknown

Taco Salad

1 (8-ounce) bottle Thousand Island
    salad dressing
1/3 cup sugar
1 envelope taco seasoning mix
1 pound ground beef
1 onion, chopped

2 or 3 tomatoes, chopped
1 head lettuce, torn into
    bite-size pieces
1/2 (13-ounce) package
    Doritos, crushed
8 ounces Cheddar cheese, shredded

Combine the salad dressing, sugar and 1 tablespoon of the taco seasoning mix in a small bowl and mix well. Brown the ground beef, onion and remaining taco seasoning mix in a skillet, stirring until the ground beef is crumbly. Combine the ground beef mixture, tomatoes, lettuce, Doritos and cheese in a large bowl and toss to mix. Add the salad dressing mixture and toss to coat. **Serves 4.**

Contributed by Debi Baron

Spinach Salad

1 pound fresh spinach
16 ounces (about) cottage cheese
1/2 cup chopped pecans
1/2 cup sour cream or plain yogurt
1/2 cup sugar
3 tablespoons cider vinegar

1 tablespoon horseradish
1/2 teaspoon dry mustard
1/2 teaspoon salt
4 slices bacon, crisp-cooked
    and crumbled

Rinse the spinach and pat dry. Tear the spinach into bite-size pieces and place in a large salad bowl. Add the cottage cheese and pecans and toss to mix. Add the sour cream and toss to mix. Combine the sugar, vinegar, horseradish, dry mustard and salt in a bowl and blend well. Pour over the spinach mixture and toss to coat. Sprinkle with the bacon. You may add 2 chopped hard-cooked eggs. **Serves 6.**

Contributed by Joann Powers

Fumi Salad

SWEET-AND-SOUR DRESSING
3/4 cup rice vinegar
1 cup olive oil
1/4 cup sugar
1 teaspoon pepper
1 teaspoon minced garlic
Salt to taste

SALAD
3 (3-ounce) packages ramen noodles
1 head red cabbage, shredded
5 green onions, sliced
1/2 cup slivered almonds, toasted
1/2 cup sesame seeds, toasted

To prepare the dressing, combine the vinegar, olive oil, sugar, pepper, garlic and salt in a bowl and mix well. Chill, covered, in the refrigerator for 8 to 10 hours.

To prepare the salad, crush the ramen noodles, reserving the seasoning packets for another purpose. Combine the cabbage, green onions, almonds and sesame seeds in a large salad bowl and toss to mix. Add the dressing and toss to coat. Sprinkle with the crushed ramen noodles and serve immediately. **Serves 6.**

Contributed by Sandy Malposuto

Broccoli Salad

3/4 cup mayonnaise
2 tablespoons white wine vinegar
1/4 cup sugar
Florets of 1 bunch broccoli

1/4 cup chopped red onion
8 to 10 slices bacon, cooked
    and crumbled
1 cup sunflower seeds

Mix the mayonnaise, vinegar and sugar in a small bowl. Combine the broccoli and onion in a bowl. Add the dressing and toss to coat. Add the bacon and sunflower seeds and toss to mix just before serving. **Serves 8.**

Contributed by Krista Borschnack

Salad Casoli

2 pounds whole green beans, cooked
1 pint cherry tomatoes, cut into halves
1 bunch green onions, sliced
2 (8-ounce) jars marinated artichoke hearts
1 medium can black olives
1 (14-ounce) can hearts of palm, sliced
1 (8-ounce) bottle zesty Italian salad dressing

Combine the green beans, tomatoes, green onions, artichoke hearts, olives and
hearts of palm in a large bowl and toss to mix. Add the salad dressing and toss
to coat. Chill, covered, in the refrigerator. **Serves 4 to 6.**

Contributed by Debi Baron

Pasta Salad

1 pound rotini
$^1/_4$ cup Italian salad dressing
$^1/_2$ cup Salad Supreme seasoning
$^1/_2$ bunch green onions, trimmed and chopped
$^1/_2$ green bell pepper, chopped
Sliced olives (optional)
Chopped cucumber (optional)
Chopped tomatoes (optional)

Cook the pasta in a large saucepan using the package directions. Drain and rinse in
cold water. Combine the pasta and salad dressing in a large container and toss to coat.
Add the Salad Supreme seasoning and stir to mix well. Cover and marinate in the
refrigerator for 8 to 10 hours. Stir in the green onions, bell pepper, olives, cucumber
and tomatoes before serving. **Serves 8 to 10.**

Contributed by Kathy Kinmonth

Strawberry and Feta Salad

1 cup slivered almonds
2 garlic cloves, minced
1 teaspoon honey
1 teaspoon Dijon mustard
1/4 cup raspberry vinegar
2 tablespoons balsamic vinegar

2 tablespoons brown sugar
1/2 cup olive oil
1/2 cup vegetable oil
1 head romaine, torn
1 pint fresh strawberries or raspberries
1 cup crumbled feta cheese

Cook the almonds in a nonstick skillet over medium heat until lightly toasted, stirring frequently. Remove from the heat and set aside. Whisk the garlic, honey, Dijon mustard, raspberry vinegar, balsamic vinegar, brown sugar, olive oil and vegetable oil in a small bowl. Combine the romaine, strawberries, feta cheese and almonds in a large bowl and toss to mix. Add the desired amount of the vinaigrette just before serving and toss to coat. You can also use spring greens, Boston lettuce or a combination of any lettuce. **Serves 4 to 6.**

Contributed by Jane Koehler

Sunset Salad

1 cup olive oil
1/2 cup sugar
1/3 cup white or red wine vinegar
1 teaspoon Dijon mustard
1 teaspoon finely chopped onion
1 tablespoon poppy seeds

Mixed salad greens
1 cup cashews
1 cup (4 ounces) shredded
    Swiss cheese
2 Gala or Fuji apples, chopped

Whisk the olive oil, sugar, vinegar, Dijon mustard, onion and poppy seeds in a large bowl until emulsified. Add the salad greens and toss to coat. Divide the salad greens equally among four to six salad plates. Sprinkle with the cashews, cheese and apples and serve immediately. **Serves 4 to 6.**

Contributed by Kerri Lilienthal

Winter Fruit Salad

1/2 cup sugar
1/3 cup lemon juice
2 teaspoons finely chopped onion
1/2 teaspoon salt
1 tablespoon poppy seeds
2/3 cup vegetable oil
1 cup (4 ounces) shredded Swiss cheese

1 large head lettuce, torn,
   or 1 package torn lettuce
1 cup chopped pecans
1/4 to 1/2 cup sweetened dried
   cranberries
1 red apple, cored and chopped
1 red pear, cored and chopped

Whisk the sugar, lemon juice, onion, salt, poppy seeds and oil in a small bowl until emulsified. Combine the cheese, lettuce, pecans, cranberries, apple and pear in a large bowl and toss to mix. Add the dressing and toss to coat. **Serves 6.**

Contributed by Joann Powers

Spinach Salad with Pecans

6 to 8 bunches small-leaf spinach,
   stems removed
1 bunch green onions, thinly sliced
1/2 cup olive oil
1/4 cup extra-virgin olive oil

1/3 cup balsamic vinegar
Salt and freshly ground pepper to taste
2 cups pecans, toasted
3 pears, cored and sliced (optional)

Rinse the spinach leaves and pat dry. (You should have 18 cups loosely packed spinach leaves. You may store the spinach leaves in a sealable plastic bag in the refrigerator for several hours at this point.) Combine the spinach and green onions in a large salad bowl and toss to mix. Whisk the olive oil, extra-virgin olive oil, vinegar, salt and pepper in a small bowl. Toss the pecans with 1/2 cup of the vinaigrette in a small bowl. Add the pecans and pears to the spinach mixture and toss to mix. Add the remaining vinaigrette and toss to coat. Serve immediately. You may peel the pears, if desired. **Serves 12.**

Contributed by Kerri Lilienthal

Strawberry and Kiwifruit Spinach Salad

1 (9-ounce) package spinach
1 quart strawberries, sliced
1 cup pecan halves, coarsely chopped
2 or 3 kiwifruit, cut into slices
   and halved

1/4 red onion, chopped
1 (8-ounce) bottle raspberry balsamic
   salad dressing
5 ounces Parmesan cheese, shredded

Combine the spinach, strawberries, pecans, kiwifruit and red onion in a large bowl and toss to mix. Add the salad dressing and toss to coat. Sprinkle the cheese over the top. **Serves 4 to 6.**

Contributed by Debi Baron

Strawberry Spinach Salad

1/2 cup sugar
11/2 teaspoons minced onion
1/4 teaspoon Worcestershire sauce
1/4 teaspoon paprika
1/4 cup cider vinegar
1/2 cup vegetable oil

1 tablespoon sesame seeds
1 tablespoon poppy seeds
1 pound spinach leaves, rinsed
   and torn
1 quart strawberries, cut into quarters

Process the sugar, onion, Worcestershire sauce, paprika and vinegar in a blender. Add the oil gradually, processing constantly until emulsified. Stir in the sesame seeds and poppy seeds. Chill in the refrigerator. Combine the spinach and strawberries in a salad bowl and toss to mix. Add the dressing and toss to coat. The salad dressing may also be served on the side. The salad dressing may be doubled and stored in an airtight container in the refrigerator. **Serves 6 to 8.**

Contributed by Vickie Shreffler

Strawberry Pecan Spinach Salad

1/2 cup vegetable oil
1/2 cup red wine vinegar
1/2 cup sugar
1/2 teaspoon dry mustard
1 (10-ounce) package spinach,
    stems removed

1 pint strawberries, sliced
1/2 cup pecans
4 to 6 green onion
    bulbs, chopped

Combine the oil, vinegar, sugar and dry mustard in a jar with a tight-fitting lid. Seal the jar and shake well. Combine the spinach, strawberries, pecans and green onions in a large salad bowl and toss to mix. Add the salad dressing and toss to coat. **Serves 4 to 6.**

Contributed by Sherri Crawford

Cherry Salad Supreme

1 (3-ounce) package raspberry gelatin
1 cup boiling water
1 (21-ounce) can cherry pie filling
1 (3-ounce) package lemon gelatin
1 cup boiling water

3 ounces cream cheese, cut into cubes
1 (8-ounce) can crushed pineapple
8 ounces whipped topping
1 cup miniature marshmallows
2 tablespoons chopped nuts

Dissolve the raspberry gelatin in 1 cup boiling water. Stir in the pie filling. Pour into a 9×9-inch dish and chill until set. Dissolve the lemon gelatin in 1 cup boiling water. Stir in the cream cheese. Let stand until cool. Stir in the undrained pineapple. Fold in the whipped topping and marshmallows. Spread over the cherry layer and sprinkle with the nuts. Chill until set. **Serves 12.**

This salad is great served for the holidays.

Contributed by Jackie Ludwig

Service to youth is the rent we pay for the space we occupy on earth. —Jane Deeter Rippin

Dad's Bean Salad

1 cup vinegar
1 cup water
2 cups sugar
1 (15-ounce) can wax beans, drained
1 (15-ounce) can butter beans, drained
1 (15-ounce) can kidney beans, rinsed and drained
1 (15-ounce) can lima beans, drained
1 (14-ounce) can green beans, drained
1 large green bell pepper, diced
1 large onion, finely chopped
3 ribs celery, diced
Salt and pepper to taste

Bring the vinegar, water and sugar to a boil in a medium saucepan over medium heat, stirring until the sugar is dissolved. Simmer for 10 minutes, stirring occasionally. Remove from the heat to cool. Combine the wax beans, butter beans, kidney beans, lima beans, green beans, bell pepper, onion and celery in a large bowl and mix well. Pour the cooled vinegar mixture over the bean mixture. Season with salt and pepper. Marinate in the refrigerator for 2 to 24 hours. This recipe is best made the night before. The recipe can be doubled by using 2 cans of each kind of bean and doubling the amount of bell pepper, onion and celery. There is no need to double the vinegar mixture. **Serves 6 to 8.**

This recipe has been in my family for over 50 years. My dad always made it for our Sunday picnics and various family events. He was very precise about how the bell pepper, onion and celery were diced and chopped. It is a refreshing salad—tried and true. He passed away when I was 13 years old, but in the years he was alive he taught me many life skills, cooking being one of them. He would be proud to know that I was sharing this recipe.

Contributed by Jane Koehler

Orange Tapioca Salad

3 cups hot water
2 (3-ounce) packages cook-and-serve
  tapioca
1 (3-ounce) package orange gelatin

8 ounces whipped topping
1 (8-ounce) can mandarin
  oranges, drained

Combine the water and tapioca in a saucepan. Bring to a boil and reduce the heat. Simmer for 1 to 2 minutes or until thickened, stirring constantly. Remove from the heat and stir in the gelatin. Let stand until cool. Fold in the whipped topping and mandarin oranges. Spoon into a serving dish. Chill, covered, for 3 to 10 hours. This recipe may be doubled. **Serves 8.**

Try this recipe using other flavors of gelatin. For Strawberry Tapioca Salad use strawberry gelatin and serve with fresh strawberries spooned over the top.

Contributed by Vickie Shreffler

Hawaiian Salad

1 (11-ounce) can mandarin oranges,
  drained, or 2 (8-ounce) cans
  mandarin oranges, drained
1 (20-ounce) can chunk
  pineapple, drained
1 (4-ounce) jar maraschino cherries,
  cut into halves

1 small package shredded coconut
  (2 cups)
1 small package miniature
  marshmallows
1 cup sour cream

Combine the mandarin oranges, pineapple, cherries, coconut, marshmallows and sour cream in a bowl and stir to mix. Chill, covered, in the refrigerator. **Serves 4.**

Contributed by Debi Baron

Main Dishes

Children of Bourbonnais Statue

Dr. A. L. Small House circa 1910

Fillet of Beef with Mustard Herb Crust

1/4 cup whole grain mustard
3 tablespoons extra-virgin olive oil
1 tablespoon finely crumbled dried savory
1 tablespoon finely crumbled dried thyme
1 whole fillet of beef (7 to 8 pounds, untrimmed,
    or 5 to 6 pounds, trimmed)
Coarse salt
Vegetable oil
Freshly ground pepper

Mix the whole grain mustard, olive oil, savory and thyme in a small bowl. Trim the beef of all excess fat. Cut the beef into two equal pieces about 7 inches long. Pat the beef dry and season generously with salt.

Heat a heavy roasting pan or skillet over medium-high heat. Pour in enough vegetable oil to just cover the bottom of the pan. Place the beef in the pan and sear for 4 minutes on each side. Remove the beef to a cutting board. Brush with the mustard mixture and generously sprinkle with pepper.

Place the beef on a rack in the roasting pan. Roast at 450 degrees for 20 minutes or to 120 degrees on a meat thermometer for medium-rare. Remove from the oven and let stand in a warm area for 15 minutes before slicing. Serve warm or at room temperature. **Serves 8 to 10.**

Contributed by Arlene Moore

Slow-Cooker Italian Beef

1 (3-pound) beef rump roast
1 (12-ounce) can beer
1 envelope Italian salad dressing mix
1 or 2 garlic cloves
1 beef bouillon cube
Hard rolls

Place the beef in a slow cooker. Add the beer, salad dressing mix, garlic and bouillon cube. Cook on High for 5 to 10 hours or until tender. Drain the beef, reserving the broth. Chill the beef and broth separately in the refrigerator. Cut the beef into very thin slices and return to the slow cooker. Skim the fat from the broth and pour the broth over the beef. Cook on Low for 1 hour. Serve on hard rolls. **Serves 10.**

Contributed by Krista Borschnack

The two biggest sellers in any bookstore are the cookbooks and the diet books. The cookbooks tell you how to prepare the food and the diet books tell you how not to eat any of it.
—Andy Rooney (TV personality and author)

Texas Beef Brisket

1 (3- to 4-pound) beef brisket
3 tablespoons liquid smoke
1 tablespoon celery salt
1 tablespoon onion salt
1 teaspoon garlic salt
Few dashes of Worcestershire sauce
Salt and cracked pepper to taste

Line a 9×13-inch baking pan with foil, leaving enough foil hanging over each side to wrap the beef. Place the beef in the prepared pan. Sprinkle with the liquid smoke, celery salt, onion salt, garlic salt, Worcestershire sauce, salt and pepper. Wrap the beef tightly in the foil. Bake at 350 degrees for 2 hours. Chill in the refrigerator for 8 to 10 hours.

Unwrap the beef carefully. Remove the beef to a cutting board, leaving the juices in the foil in the pan. Cut the beef into thin slices and return to the juices in the foil. Rewrap the beef tightly and bake at 350 degrees for 2 hours. Do not use corned beef brisket in this recipe. **Serves 8 to 10.**

Contributed by Sarah Bowman-Steffes

Slow-Cooker Beef Goulash

¼ cup all-purpose flour
Dash of pepper
1 pound beef stew meat
1 small onion, sliced
2 garlic cloves, minced
1 (28-ounce) can diced tomatoes
1 (6-ounce) can tomato paste
1 cup water
2 tablespoons brown sugar
1 tablespoon paprika
1 teaspoon marjoram
Hot cooked rice or noodles

Mix the flour and pepper in a bowl. Add the beef and toss to coat. Combine the beef mixture, onion, garlic, undrained tomatoes, tomato paste, water, brown sugar, paprika and marjoram in a slow cooker and mix well. Cook on Low for 8 to 12 hours. Serve over hot cooked rice or noodles. This recipe may be doubled and freezes well. **Serves 4 to 6.**

Contributed by Gail Passwater

There is no such thing as a little garlic. —Arthur "Bugs" Baer (Journalist and cartoonist)

Slow-Cooker Beef Stew

1½ pounds beef stew meat
2 ribs celery, sliced
4 carrots, sliced
3 or 4 potatoes, peeled and cut into cubes
1 envelope onion soup mix
3 (10-ounce) cans tomato soup
1 garlic clove, crushed
Salt and pepper to taste
2 tablespoons cornstarch
¼ cup cold water

Brown the beef in a nonstick skillet. Combine the beef, celery, carrots and potatoes in a slow cooker. Mix the onion soup mix, tomato soup, garlic, salt and pepper in a bowl. Pour over the beef mixture and mix well. Cook on Low for 8 to 10 hours. Dissolve the cornstarch in the water. Add to the beef mixture and mix well. Cook on High until thickened. **Serves 8.**

Contributed by Allison Beasley

Ground Beef Casserole

1 1/2 pounds ground beef
1 cup chopped onion
1 1/2 cups frozen whole kernel corn
1 (10-ounce) can cream of mushroom soup
1 (10-ounce) can cream of chicken soup
1 cup sour cream
1/2 cup chopped pimentos
3/4 teaspoon salt
1/4 teaspoon pepper
3 cups medium egg noodles, cooked
1 cup buttered bread crumbs

Brown the ground beef with the onion in a skillet, stirring until the ground beef is crumbly; drain. Add the corn, mushroom soup, chicken soup, sour cream, pimentos, salt and pepper and mix well. Stir in the noodles. Spoon into a baking dish and top with the bread crumbs. Bake at 350 degrees for 30 minutes. You may prepare ahead and freeze. **Serves 5 or 6.**

Contributed by Jackie Ludwig

Ground Beef Surprise

1 pound ground beef
1 small onion, chopped
1 cup spaghetti sauce
1¹/₂ cups (6 ounces) shredded mozzarella cheese
¹/₃ cup sour cream
1 (8-count) can refrigerator crescent rolls
2 tablespoons butter or margarine
Grated Parmesan cheese

Brown the ground beef with the onion in a skillet, stirring until the ground beef is crumbly; drain. Stir in the spaghetti sauce. Spoon into a 9×9-inch baking pan. Mix the mozzarella cheese and sour cream in a bowl. Spread over the ground beef layer. Unroll the crescent roll dough, pressing the perforations to seal. Place over the cheese layer. Spread the top with the butter and sprinkle with Parmesan cheese. Bake at 375 degrees for 18 to 25 minutes or until brown on top. **Serves 4.**

Contributed by Jen Yohnka

In the childhood memories of every good cook, there's a large kitchen, a warm stove, a simmering pot, and a mom. —Barbara Costikayn

Karen's Ground Beef and Noodle Casserole

1 pound ground beef
$1/4$ cup water
1 onion, chopped
1 green bell pepper, chopped
Salt and pepper to taste
1 (10-ounce) can cream of mushroom soup
1 (10-ounce) can tomato soup
$1/4$ to $1/2$ cup (1 to 2 ounces) grated Parmesan cheese
8 ounces egg noodles, cooked
2 cups (8 ounces) shredded mozzarella cheese

Brown the ground beef in a skillet, stirring until crumbly. Drain the ground beef and return to the skillet. Add the water, onion and bell pepper and mix well. Simmer for 10 minutes. Season with salt and pepper.

Combine the mushroom soup, tomato soup and Parmesan cheese in a large bowl and mix well. Stir in the ground beef mixture. Fold in the egg noodles. Spoon into a baking dish and sprinkle with the mozzarella cheese. Bake at 350 degrees for 45 minutes. **Serves 6.**

Contributed by Karen Johnston-Gentry

Pizza Casserole

1 pound ground beef
2 cups cooked wide egg noodles
1 (14-ounce) jar pizza sauce
3 ounces pepperoni slices
1 (4-ounce) can mushrooms, drained
2 cups (8 ounces) shredded mozzarella cheese
1 cup (4 ounces) shredded Cheddar cheese

Brown the ground beef in a skillet, stirring until crumbly; drain. Add the noodles, pizza sauce, pepperoni and mushrooms and mix well. Spoon into a 9×13-inch baking dish sprayed with nonstick cooking spray. Sprinkle with the mozzarella cheese and Cheddar cheese. Bake at 350 degrees for 30 minutes. **Serves 6 to 8.**

Contributed by Sandy Malposuto

I cook with wine…sometimes I even put it in food. —Unknown

Microwave Pizza Meat Loaf

1 1/2 pounds ground beef
1 egg, lightly beaten
1/2 cup bread crumbs
1 (8-ounce) can pizza sauce
3/4 teaspoon Italian seasoning
1/2 teaspoon oregano
1/4 teaspoon salt
1/4 teaspoon pepper
2 cups (8 ounces) shredded mozzarella cheese

Combine the ground beef, egg, bread crumbs, 1/4 cup of the pizza sauce, the Italian seasoning, oregano, salt and pepper in a large mixing bowl and mix well. Shape into a 10×12-inch rectangle on waxed paper. Sprinkle 1 1/2 cups of the cheese over the rectangle. Roll up to enclose the cheese, beginning at the narrow end and sealing the edges well. Place seam side down in a 1 1/2-quart microwave-safe dish.

Microwave on High for 6 minutes. Pour the remaining 3/4 cup pizza sauce over the meat loaf. Microwave on Medium for 30 to 35 minutes or to 160 degrees on a meat thermometer, sprinkling with the remaining 1/2 cup cheese during the last 5 minutes. **Serves 4 to 6.**

Contributed by Missie Rolinitis

"Souper" Meat and Potatoes Pie

1 pound ground beef
1 (10-ounce) can cream of mushroom soup
1/4 cup chopped onion
1 egg, lightly beaten
1/4 cup fine dry bread crumbs
1/4 teaspoon salt
Dash of pepper
2 cups mashed potatoes
1/4 cup (1 ounce) shredded Cheddar cheese

Brown the ground beef in a skillet, stirring until crumbly; drain. Add 1/2 cup of the soup, onion, egg, bread crumbs, salt and pepper and mix well. (Reserve the remaining soup for another use.) Press firmly into a 9-inch pie plate. Bake at 350 degrees for 25 minutes. Spread the mashed potatoes over the top and sprinkle with the cheese. Bake for 10 minutes. **Serves 6.**

Contributed by Krista Borschnack

Never eat more than you can lift. —Miss Piggy

Tex-Mex Beef Tacos

1 pound ground sirloin
1 cup chopped onion
1 garlic clove, minced
1 cup frozen whole kernel corn
1/2 cup water
1/4 teaspoon salt
1/8 teaspoon pepper
1 (15-ounce) can black beans, rinsed and drained
1 (8-ounce) can tomato sauce
1 (4-ounce) can green chiles
8 to 10 flour tortillas, warmed

Heat a large skillet over medium-high heat. Coat the hot skillet with nonstick cooking spray. Brown the ground sirloin with the onion and garlic in the prepared skillet, stirring until the ground sirloin is crumbly; drain. Stir in the corn, water, salt, pepper, black beans, tomato sauce and green chiles. Bring to a boil and reduce the heat. Simmer for 10 minutes. Spoon onto each tortilla. Serve with shredded cheese, shredded lettuce and sour cream. **Makes 8 to 10 tacos.**

For nachos, serve the filling over tortilla chips. For a tasty taco salad, serve the filling over a bed of lettuce.

Contributed by Jackie Ludwig

Bowman Beanie Weenies

1 (16-ounce) package beef frankfurters,
    thinly sliced
1 roll Italian sausage or spicy hot sausage,
    casings removed and sausage finely chopped
1 (18-ounce) bottle thick and spicy original
    barbecue sauce
1 (28-ounce) can original baked beans
Salt and pepper to taste

Sauté the frankfurters in a nonstick skillet until brown and cooked through. Combine
the frankfurters, Italian sausage, barbecue sauce and baked beans in a large saucepan
or slow cooker and mix well. Cook for 15 to 30 minutes or until the sausage is cooked
through. Season with salt and pepper. **Serves 4 to 6.**

*No onions! This easy recipe was created for people who love baked beans but don't like onions.
It can also be served as a side dish with brisket or steak.*

Contributed by Sarah Bowman-Steffes

Pork Roast with Peach Sauce

1 (3-pound) boneless pork loin roast, tied
1/4 teaspoon onion salt
1/4 teaspoon pepper
1 (15-ounce) can sliced peaches
1/2 cup chili sauce
1/3 cup packed light brown sugar
3 tablespoons apple cider vinegar
1 teaspoon pumpkin pie spice
1 tablespoon cornstarch
2 tablespoons water

Place the pork in a 6-quart slow cooker sprayed with nonstick cooking spray. Season with the onion salt and pepper. Drain the peaches, reserving the syrup. Whisk the reserved syrup, chili sauce, brown sugar, vinegar and pumpkin pie spice in a bowl. Pour over the pork. Scatter with the peaches. Cook on High for 3 hours or on Low for 6 hours.

Remove the pork to a cutting board and let stand for 10 minutes. Remove the peach slices with a slotted spoon to a bowl. Pour the liquid into a small saucepan and bring to a boil over medium-high heat. Stir in a mixture of the cornstarch and water. Cook until thickened, stirring constantly. Cut the pork into slices and place on a serving platter. Scatter the peaches over the pork. Serve with the sauce and with hot cooked egg noodles, if desired. **Serves 8.**

Contributed by Melissa Fischer

Mom's Ham Barbecue

1/4 cup (1/2 stick) margarine
2 cups chili sauce
3/4 cup ketchup
Water
1 teaspoon white vinegar
1 cup packed brown sugar
1 to 2 teaspoons Worcestershire sauce
1 teaspoon mustard
5 pounds shaved ham

Melt the margarine in a large skillet. Stir in the chili sauce and ketchup. Add enough water to the measuring cups to rinse out all of the chili sauce and ketchup and pour into the skillet. Stir in the vinegar, brown sugar, Worcestershire sauce and mustard. Add the ham gradually, stirring to coat evenly. Simmer for at least 45 minutes before serving. **Makes enough for 30 to 36 sandwiches.**

Contributed by Debi Baron

A gourmet who thinks of calories is like a tart who looks at her watch. —James Beard

Black Bean Chili

6 tablespoons olive oil
1 (12-ounce) onion, coarsely chopped (about 3 cups)
1 large yellow bell pepper, chopped
1¹/2 tablespoons cumin seeds
4 teaspoons minced canned chipotle chiles
3 (15-ounce) cans black beans, drained
2 (14-ounce) cans diced tomatoes with roasted garlic
2 cups vegetable broth
Salt and pepper to taste

Heat the olive oil in a large heavy saucepan over medium-high heat. Add the onion, bell pepper and cumin seeds. Sauté for 10 minutes or until the onion is tender and golden brown. Add the chiles and sauté for 30 seconds. Add the black beans, undrained tomatoes and broth. Bring to a boil and reduce the heat to medium. Simmer for 30 minutes or until the liquid is reduced by half, stirring occasionally. Process 2 cups of the mixture in a food processor to form a coarse paste. Return to the saucepan and mix well. Simmer until thickened, if desired. Season with salt and pepper. Ladle into soup bowls and garnish with sour cream and shredded cheese. You may make 1 day ahead and store, covered, in the refrigerator. Frozen corn may be added.
Serves 8.

Contributed by Lisa Joubert

White Bean Chicken Chili

1 tablespoon olive oil
1 small onion, finely chopped
2 garlic cloves, finely chopped
1 red bell pepper, finely chopped
2 (15-ounce) cans white beans
1 (4-ounce) can diced green chiles
1 teaspoon chili powder
1/2 teaspoon cumin
1 (14-ounce) can low-sodium chicken broth
8 ounces roasted chicken breasts,
     cut into 1/2-inch cubes
2 tablespoons minced cilantro (optional)
6 tablespoons salsa (optional)
11/2 cups (6 ounces) shredded Monterey Jack
     cheese (optional)

Heat the olive oil in a large saucepan over medium heat. Add the onion, garlic and bell pepper and sauté for 5 minutes. Stir in the undrained white beans, green chiles, chili powder, cumin and broth. Bring to a boil and reduce the heat. Simmer for 10 minutes. Stir in the chicken and simmer for 5 minutes. Stir in the cilantro. Ladle into soup bowls and top with the salsa and cheese. **Serves 6 to 8.**

Contributed by Kerri Lilienthal

Chicken Bulgogi

2 cups soy sauce
2 tablespoons sesame oil
1/4 cup sesame seeds, roasted
2 tablespoons brown sugar
1 teaspoon garlic powder
1 garlic clove, crushed
2 green onion stems, sliced
6 boneless skinless chicken breasts

Combine the soy sauce, sesame oil, sesame seeds, brown sugar, garlic powder, garlic and green onions in a large glass bowl and mix well. Add the chicken. Marinate in the refrigerator for 1 hour. Drain the chicken, discarding the marinade. Place the chicken on a grill rack and grill over low heat for 15 to 20 minutes on each side or until cooked through. Serve hot. **Serves 6 to 8.**

Contributed by Rochelle McAvoy

You may not have saved a lot of money in your life, but if you have saved a lot of heartaches for other folks, you are a pretty rich man. —Seth Parker

Chicken Parmigiana

1 cup bread crumbs
1/4 cup (1 ounce) grated
    Parmesan cheese
1 teaspoon dried basil or
    dried oregano
1 teaspoon salt
1/2 teaspoon pepper
2 eggs
2 tablespoons water
1/4 cup all-purpose flour

4 to 6 thin slices chicken breasts
1/3 cup olive oil
11/2 cups basil-flavored
    pasta sauce
3 to 4 tablespoons grated
    Parmesan cheese
4 to 6 slices mozzarella cheese
1/4 cup (1 ounce) grated
    Parmesan cheese
1/8 teaspoon dried basil

Mix the bread crumbs, 1/4 cup Parmesan cheese, 1 teaspoon basil, the salt and pepper in a shallow dish. Whisk the eggs and water in a small bowl. Spread the flour on a plate. Coat the chicken with the flour. Dip in the egg mixture and coat with the bread crumb mixture. Cook the chicken in the hot olive oil in a skillet for 2 to 3 minutes on each side or until light brown. Remove from the skillet and blot with paper towels.

Spoon 1/2 cup of the pasta sauce into a 9×13-inch baking dish sprayed with nonstick cooking spray. Arrange the chicken slightly overlapping in the sauce. Sprinkle with 3 to 4 tablespoons Parmesan cheese. Spoon the remaining 1 cup pasta sauce over the chicken. Layer the mozzarella cheese over the top. Sprinkle with 1/4 cup Parmesan cheese and 1/8 teaspoon basil. Cover with foil and bake at 350 degrees for 10 to 15 minutes or until cooked through. **Serves 4 to 6.**

Contributed by Melissa Fischer

Chicken Tarragon

6 boneless skinless chicken breasts
2 tablespoons butter
Salt and pepper to taste
1 tablespoon finely chopped
 green onions
1 tablespoon butter
1/4 cup dry white vermouth

1 teaspoon dried tarragon
1 beef bouillon cube
1/4 cup water
1 cup whipping cream
1 tablespoon cornstarch
1 tablespoon water
Chopped parsley

Pound the chicken with a meat mallet to flatten. Sauté the chicken in 2 tablespoons butter in a skillet for 4 to 5 minutes on each side. Place in a baking dish and season with salt and pepper.

Sauté the green onions in 1 tablespoon butter in a skillet. Stir in the vermouth, tarragon, bouillon cube, 1/4 cup water and the whipping cream. Bring to a boil and cook until the liquid is reduced by two-thirds. Mix the cornstarch with 1 tablespoon water in a small cup and add to the sauce. Cook until the sauce is thickened to the desired consistency, stirring constantly. Pour over the chicken.

Bake at 350 degrees for 20 to 25 minutes or until the chicken is cooked through. Sprinkle with parsley and serve. **Serves 6.**

Contributed by Leslie Geoffrey

Hot Chicken Salad Casserole

3 cups cubed cooked chicken
1¹/₂ cups chopped celery
1 cup sliced water chestnuts
3 cups (12 ounces) shredded Cheddar cheese
3 tablespoons lemon juice
¹/₂ teaspoon salt
1¹/₂ cups mayonnaise
1 (10-ounce) can cream of chicken soup
¹/₄ cup (1 ounce) shredded Cheddar cheese
1¹/₂ cups crushed potato chips
Hot bread or lettuce leaves

Combine the chicken, celery, water chestnuts, 3 cups cheese, the lemon juice, salt, mayonnaise and soup in a bowl and mix well. Spoon into a large baking dish. Sprinkle with ¹/₄ cup cheese and the potato chips. Bake at 325 degrees for 45 minutes. Serve on hot bread or lettuce. **Serves 6 to 8.**

Contributed by Jackie Ludwig

Mexican Chicken Casserole

1 (14-ounce) can chicken broth
2 (4-ounce) cans chopped green chiles
4 boneless skinless chicken breasts
1 onion, chopped
2 teaspoons olive oil
1 cup evaporated milk
2 ounces cream cheese, softened
1 cup (4 ounces) shredded Monterey Jack cheese
1 (10-ounce) can enchilada sauce
12 (6-inch) corn tortillas or flour tortillas
1/2 cup (2 ounces) shredded Cheddar cheese

Bring the broth and green chiles to a boil in a large skillet. Add the chicken and cook for 15 minutes or until cooked through. Remove the chicken to a plate and shred. Sauté the onion in the olive oil in a small skillet until translucent. Add the sautéed onion to the liquid in the large skillet and simmer for 3 minutes. Stir in the evaporated milk, cream cheese, Monterey Jack cheese and enchilada sauce. Return the chicken to the skillet and cook for 2 minutes.

Layer one-third of the tortillas and one-third of the chicken mixture in a greased 9×13-inch baking dish. Repeat the layers twice, ending with the chicken mixture. Sprinkle with the Cheddar cheese. Bake at 350 degrees for 30 minutes. **Serves 4 to 6.**

Contributed by Sherri Crawford

Southwest Egg Rolls

1 boneless skinless chicken breast
2 tablespoons vegetable oil
2 tablespoons minced green onions
2 tablespoons minced red bell pepper
1/3 cup frozen corn kernels
1/4 cup black beans, rinsed and drained
2 tablespoons drained thawed frozen
    chopped spinach
2 tablespoons chopped jalapeño chiles

1 tablespoon minced fresh parsley
1/2 teaspoon cumin
1/2 teaspoon chili powder
1/2 teaspoon salt
Pinch of cayenne pepper
3/4 cup (3 ounces) shredded Monterey
    Jack cheese
5 (6-inch) flour tortillas
Vegetable oil for deep-frying

Cook the chicken in 1 tablespoon of the oil in a skillet for 5 minutes on each side or until cooked through. Remove the chicken from the skillet and set aside. Heat the remaining 1 tablespoon oil in the skillet over medium heat. Add the green onions and bell pepper and sauté for 5 minutes. Shred or chop the chicken and return to the skillet. Add the corn, black beans, spinach, jalapeño chiles, parsley, cumin, chili powder, salt and cayenne pepper. Cook for 5 minutes or until tender, stirring to blend. Remove from the heat. Stir in the Monterey Jack cheese until melted.

Wrap the tortillas in a moist microwave-safe cloth. Microwave on High for 1 minute. Spoon about 1/3 cup of the chicken mixture onto each tortilla. Fold in the ends and roll up tightly, securing with wooden picks. Freeze, covered, for 4 to 10 hours.

To serve, deep-fry the frozen egg rolls in 375-degree oil in a deep fryer for 6 to 8 minutes or until golden brown. Drain on paper towels. **Serves 5.**

Contributed by Lisa Kick

Gourmet Chicken à la King in Minutes

1 small package mushrooms, cut into halves
1 green bell pepper, sliced
1 onion, sliced
1/4 cup (1/2 stick) butter
1 purchased roasted chicken, sliced
1 (10-ounce) can cream of mushroom soup
1/2 cup milk
Toasted bread

Sauté the mushrooms, bell pepper and onion in the butter until tender. Add the chicken and cook until heated through. Stir in the soup and milk. Cook until heated through. Serve over toasted bread and garnish with pimento and almond slices. **Serves 4.**

Contributed by Kim Donald

Those who can, do. Those who can do more, volunteer. —Author unknown

Chicken Squares

3 ounces cream cheese, softened
2 tablespoons butter or margarine, melted
2 cups cubed cooked chicken
1/4 teaspoon salt
1/8 teaspoon pepper
2 tablespoons milk
1 tablespoon chopped onion
1 tablespoon chopped pimento
1 (8-count) can refrigerator crescent rolls
1 tablespoon butter or margarine, melted
Bread crumbs

Blend the cream cheese and 2 tablespoons butter in a bowl until smooth. Add the chicken, salt, pepper, milk, onion and pimento and mix well. Unroll the crescent roll dough. Separate into four rectangles and press the perforations to seal. Spoon 1/2 cup of the chicken mixture onto each rectangle. Pull up the four corners of each rectangle to the center and seal. Brush with 1 tablespoon butter and dip in bread crumbs. Place on an ungreased baking sheet and bake at 375 degrees for 20 to 25 minutes or until golden brown. **Serves 4.**

Contributed by Jen Yohnka

Barbecued Chicken Pizza

2 cups cubed cooked chicken
1/2 cup barbecue sauce
1 teaspoon chili powder
1 prebaked Italian bread shell
2 cups (8 ounces) shredded Monterey Jack cheese
1/4 cup chopped green bell pepper
1/2 cup pineapple tidbits

Combine the chicken, barbecue sauce and chili powder in a small bowl and mix well. Place the bread shell on a baking sheet and spread evenly with the chicken mixture. Sprinkle with the cheese, bell pepper and pineapple. Bake at 450 degrees for 15 minutes or until the cheese melts. **Serves 4 or 5.**

Contributed by Christine Betts

The discovery of a new dish does more for the happiness of mankind than the discovery of a star.
—Anthelme Brillat-Savarin

Chicken Potpie with Cornmeal Crust

CHICKEN FILLING
1 pound boneless chicken breasts
2 cups chicken broth
1¹/2 tablespoons vegetable oil
1 cup quartered new potatoes
1 cup baby carrots
1 cup cipollini onions, cut into quarters
1 cup (1-inch) asparagus pieces
Salt and pepper to taste
1 cup frozen peas
2 tablespoons butter
3 tablespoons all-purpose flour
2 tablespoons whipping cream

2 tablespoons chopped fresh chives
2 teaspoons fresh thyme

CORNMEAL CRUST AND ASSEMBLY
1 cup all-purpose flour
¹/2 cup cornmeal
1 teaspoon salt
¹/4 teaspoon pepper
¹/2 cup (1 stick) butter
¹/4 cup shortening
¹/3 cup ice water
1 egg
1 teaspoon water

To prepare the filling, poach the chicken in the simmering broth in a saucepan for 10 minutes or until cooked through. Remove the chicken, shred and set aside. Strain 1¹/2 cups of the broth into a liquid measure, discarding the solids, and set aside. Heat the oil in a medium skillet. Add the potatoes and cook for 4 minutes or until golden brown. Add the carrots, onions and asparagus and cook for 4 minutes or until tender. Season with salt and pepper. Combine with the chicken and peas in a large bowl and mix well. Melt the butter in a skillet over low heat. Add the flour and cook for 1 minute, stirring constantly. Whisk in the reserved broth. Cook over medium heat for 3 minutes or until thickened, whisking constantly. Stir in the cream, chives and thyme. Season with salt and pepper. Stir into the chicken mixture.

To prepare the crust, mix the flour, cornmeal, salt and pepper in a bowl. Cut in the butter and shortening with a pastry blender to form pea-sized crumbs. Add the water a small amount at a time, tossing with a fork to form a ball. Place on a work surface and knead once or twice. Shape into four thick discs.

To assemble, gently spoon the filling into four 1-cup ovenproof pie plates or bowls. Place the cornmeal discs on top of the filling. Crimp the dough over the side of the pie plates and cut a slit in the center of each. Beat the egg and water together and brush over the top. Place the pie plates on a baking sheet and bake at 400 degrees for 25 to 30 minutes or until golden brown. **Serves 4.**

Contributed by Karen Johnston-Gentry

Slow-Cooker Onion Turkey Breast

1 (4- to 6-pound) turkey breast
1 teaspoon garlic powder
1 envelope onion soup mix

Place the turkey in a slow cooker. Add the garlic powder and onion soup mix.
Cover and cook on Low for 8 to 10 hours or until the turkey is cooked through.
Serves 4.

Contributed by Tiffany Holohan

Serve this dish with too much wine for your guest, along with some good cooked green vegetables and a huge salad. You will be famous in about a half an hour. —Jeff Smith (The Frugal Gourmet)

Turkey Le Grand

16 ounces cream cheese
2 cups chicken broth or stock or
    turkey broth or stock
4 cups sour cream
Salt and pepper to taste
Poultry seasoning or Beau Monde
    seasoning to taste
2 cups steamed broccoli
2 cups cubed cooked turkey
1 (4-ounce) can mushrooms, drained
1 (8-count) can refrigerator flaky biscuits
Paprika

Microwave the cream cheese on High in a microwave-safe bowl until soft. Stir in the broth until blended. Spoon into a Dutch oven and stir in the sour cream gradually. Cook over low heat until blended, stirring constantly. Season with salt, pepper and poultry seasoning. Stir in the broccoli and turkey. Cook until heated through. Stir in the mushrooms. You may thicken the mixture if needed.

Bake the biscuits using the package directions. Cut the hot biscuits horizontally into halves. Place the bottom half of each biscuit on a serving plate. Ladle the turkey mixture over the bottom halves. Replace the top halves of the biscuits and sprinkle with paprika. **Serves 8.**

Contributed by Janice Krizik-Schmidt

Salmon Quesadillas

1 pound salmon, cooked
6 ounces cream cheese, softened
1 to 2 teaspoons dill weed
2 tablespoons minced green onions
2 garlic cloves, minced
6 (6-inch) flour tortillas
2 cups (8 ounces) shredded mozzarella cheese
Butter

Shred or chop the salmon, discarding the skin and bones. Combine the salmon and cream cheese in a skillet and heat until the cream cheese melts, stirring constantly. Add the dill weed, green onions and garlic and cook until heated through. Turn off the heat.

Scoop 1/2 cup of the salmon mixture onto one side of each tortilla and cover lightly with the mozzarella cheese. Fold over the remaining side to cover the salmon mixture. Cook in melted butter in a skillet until golden brown, turning once. Serve with salsa and sour cream. **Serves 6.**

Contributed by Ann O'Gorman

Swiss Tuna Quiche

1 (9-inch) deep-dish pie shell, thawed
1 (6-ounce) can tuna, drained
1 1/4 cups (5 ounces) shredded Swiss cheese
1/2 cup finely chopped onion
2 eggs, beaten
1 cup evaporated milk
1 tablespoon lemon juice
1 teaspoon chives
3/4 teaspoon garlic salt
1/2 teaspoon salt
1/8 teaspoon pepper

Prick the bottom and side of the pie shell with a fork. Place on a baking sheet and bake at 450 degrees for 5 minutes. Remove from the oven and maintain the oven temperature. Spread the tuna evenly over the bottom of the partially baked pie shell. Sprinkle with the cheese and onion. Whisk the eggs, evaporated milk, lemon juice, chives, garlic salt, salt and pepper in a bowl and pour over the layers. Place on a baking sheet and bake for 15 minutes. Reduce the oven temperature to 350 degrees and bake for 15 to 18 minutes longer or until the top is golden brown. **Serves 6.**

Contributed by Jen Yohnka

Shrimp and Potatoes with Tarragon Dressing

Tarragon Dressing
1/4 cup light mayonnaise
1/4 cup buttermilk or plain
   lowfat yogurt
2 green onions, sliced
2 tablespoons parsley
1 teaspoon tarragon
1 garlic clove, minced

Shrimp and Potatoes
3 potatoes, cut into 1/4-inch-thick slices
Salt to taste
4 cups water
2 tablespoons vinegar
1/2 teaspoon salt
1 pound fresh or frozen shrimp,
   peeled and deveined
Lettuce leaves

To prepare the dressing, process the mayonnaise, buttermilk, green onions, parsley, tarragon and garlic in a blender until smooth.

To prepare the shrimp and potatoes, cook the potatoes, covered, in a small amount of lightly salted boiling water in a saucepan for 8 to 12 minutes or until tender; drain. Bring 4 cups water, the vinegar and 1/2 teaspoon salt to a boil in a large saucepan. Add the shrimp and reduce the heat. Simmer for 1 to 3 minutes or until the shrimp turn pink; drain. Rinse with cold water; drain. Arrange the potatoes and shrimp on four lettuce-lined serving plates. Drizzle the dressing over the top. Garnish with cherry tomatoes. **Serves 4.**

Contributed by Gina Shell-LaMore

Pasta Main Dishes

The Lemuel Milk Carriage House, known locally as
the Stone Barn, has served as the headquarters of the
Junior League of Kankakee County since 1976.

Schuyler Avenue
Downtown Kankakee

Garlic Asparagus and Pasta with Lemon Cream

6 ounces rotini
2 cups (2-inch) asparagus pieces
8 baby sunburst squash and/or pattypan squash,
    cut into halves
2 garlic cloves, minced
1 tablespoon butter or margarine
1 (12-ounce) can evaporated fat-free milk
1 tablespoon all-purpose flour
1/4 cup (1 ounce) grated Parmesan cheese
2 tablespoons finely shredded lemon zest

Cook the pasta using the package directions; drain. Place the pasta in a large bowl and keep warm. Sauté the asparagus, squash and garlic in the melted butter in a large skillet for 2 to 3 minutes or until the vegetables are tender-crisp. Remove with a slotted spoon and add to the pasta. Stir the evaporated milk into the flour in a medium saucepan. Cook over medium heat until thickened and bubbly, stirring constantly. Cook for 1 minute longer, stirring constantly. Stir in the cheese and lemon zest and cook until heated through. Pour over the pasta mixture and toss to coat. Serve with additional grated Parmesan cheese. You may substitute 1 medium yellow squash or zucchini, cut into 16 pieces, for the baby sunburst and/or pattypan squash. **Serves 4 to 6.**

Contributed by Gina Shell-LaMore

Creamy Asparagus Lasagna

3 tablespoons unsalted butter
3 tablespoons unbleached flour
1¹/2 cups hot milk
¹/2 teaspoon coarse kosher salt
2 tablespoons unsalted butter
1 tablespoon olive oil
1 large onion, thinly sliced
¹/2 teaspoon coarse kosher salt

2 pounds fresh asparagus, trimmed
4 teaspoons olive oil
¹/2 cup plus 1 teaspoon heavy cream
16 ounces lasagna noodles, cooked and
    drained
12 slices fresh mozzarella cheese
1¹/4 cups (5 ounces) freshly grated
    Parmesan cheese

Melt 3 tablespoons butter in a heavy medium saucepan over low heat. Stir in the flour. Cook for 1 minute or until the mixture bubbles, stirring constantly. Do not brown. Remove from the heat and gradually whisk in the milk. Return to the heat and cook for 10 minutes or until thickened, whisking constantly. Stir in ¹/2 teaspoon kosher salt and pour into a bowl. Press a piece of plastic wrap or waxed paper on the surface of the sauce and set aside.

Melt 2 tablespoons butter with 1 tablespoon olive oil in a large skillet. Add the onion and sprinkle with ¹/2 teaspoon kosher salt. Cook over low heat for 15 to 20 minutes or until the onion is tender and golden brown.

Coat the asparagus with 4 teaspoons olive oil. Place the asparagus in a single layer in a microwave-safe dish. Microwave on High for 10 minutes or until tender-crisp. Let stand until cool. Cut the asparagus diagonally into slices.

To assemble, spread 1 tablespoon of the sauce in the bottom of a baking pan and drizzle with 2 tablespoons of the cream. Cover with a layer of lasagna noodles and 2 tablespoons of the remaining sauce. Continue layering with 1 cup of the asparagus and 1 cup of the onion. Cover with a layer of mozzarella cheese and sprinkle with ¹/4 cup of the Parmesan cheese. Drizzle with 2 tablespoons of the remaining cream and cover with another layer of lasagna noodles. Repeat the layering twice, ending with the remaining lasagna noodles, remaining sauce, remaining cream and remaining Parmesan cheese. Cover loosely with foil and bake at 500 degrees for 10 minutes. Uncover and bake for 20 to 30 minutes longer or until golden brown and bubbly. Let stand for 10 minutes before serving. **Serves 4 to 6.**

Contributed by Rochelle McAvoy

Meatless Lasagna

15 ounces ricotta cheese
2 cups (8 ounces) shredded mozzarella cheese
$1/4$ cup (1 ounce) grated Parmesan cheese
2 eggs
1 teaspoon basil
1 teaspoon oregano
1 teaspoon parsley flakes
$1/2$ teaspoon garlic powder
$1/8$ teaspoon pepper
$1^1/2$ (26-ounce) jars chunky tomato, onion and garlic pasta sauce
12 lasagna noodles, cooked and drained
$1/4$ cup (1 ounce) grated Parmesan cheese

Combine the ricotta cheese, mozzarella cheese, $1/4$ cup Parmesan cheese, the eggs, basil, oregano, parsley flakes, garlic powder and pepper in a large bowl and mix well. Spread 1 cup of the pasta sauce and $1/3$ cup of the cheese mixture in a 10×14-inch baking dish. Layer the lasagna noodles, one-half of the remaining sauce and remaining cheese mixture one-half at a time in the prepared dish. Spread the remaining sauce over the top. Cover with foil and bake at 375 degrees for 30 minutes. Remove the foil and sprinkle with $1/4$ cup Parmesan cheese. Bake for 5 minutes longer. Remove from the oven and let stand for 10 minutes before serving. **Serves 10.**

Contributed by Kathy Kinmonth

Vegetable Lasagna

4 to 5 cups (¹/2-inch) vegetable slices or pieces
    (onions, carrots, zucchini, yellow squash
    and mushrooms)
4 to 5 cups tomato sauce
4 cups ricotta cheese
3 eggs, lightly beaten
2 to 3 tablespoons sugar
¹/2 cup (2 ounces) grated Parmesan cheese
8 ounces lasagna noodles
8 ounces Swiss cheese, shredded
16 ounces mozzarella cheese, shredded

Sauté the vegetables in a nonstick skillet until tender. Combine with the tomato sauce in a bowl and mix well. Mix the ricotta cheese, eggs, sugar and Parmesan cheese in a bowl. Alternate layers of the vegetable sauce, lasagna noodles, ricotta cheese mixture, vegetable sauce, Swiss cheese and mozzarella cheese in a 9×13-inch baking pan until all ingredients are used, ending with a layer of the sauce, Swiss cheese and mozzarella cheese. Bake at 350 degrees for 30 minutes or until bubbly. Let stand for 10 minutes before serving. **Serves 10 to 12.**

Contributed by Debi Baron

Spaghetti Florentine

8 ounces spaghetti
1 onion, chopped
8 to 10 ounces fresh leaf spinach
Olive oil
2 eggs
2 tablespoons butter, melted

1¼ cups (5 ounces) shredded
    mozzarella cheese
1 teaspoon salt
Freshly ground pepper to taste
¼ cup diced pimentos
3 to 4 cups spaghetti sauce

Cook the spaghetti using the package directions; drain. Sauté the onion and spinach
in a small amount of olive oil in a large skillet for 3 to 4 minutes or until tender.
Beat the eggs in a large bowl. Add the butter, cheese, salt, pepper and pimentos and
mix well. Add the spaghetti and spinach mixture and toss to mix well. Place in
a greased 2-quart baking dish and cover loosely with foil. Bake at 375 degrees for
25 to 30 minutes or until cooked through. Cut into squares and serve with the
spaghetti sauce. **Serves 8.**

Contributed by Lesley Robinson

Cold Ginger Soy and Honey Sesame Noodles

1 teaspoon light sesame seeds
    (optional)
2 teaspoons peanut butter
1 teaspoon honey
2 teaspoons tamari

1 teaspoon sesame oil
1 teaspoon ground ginger, or 1-inch
    piece fresh ginger, peeled and grated
4 ounces spaghetti, cooked, rinsed
    and drained

Spread the sesame seeds on a baking sheet. Bake at 350 degrees for 3 minutes or until
toasted. Cook the peanut butter in a microwave-safe bowl on High for 15 to
20 seconds or until melted. Whisk in the honey and tamari until smooth. Whisk in
the sesame oil and ginger. Add to the spaghetti in a large bowl and toss to coat.
Spoon into a serving bowl and sprinkle with the sesame seeds. **Serves 4.**

Contributed by Lesley Robinson

Marinara Magnifica

4 cups chopped onions (about 2)
2 teaspoons minced garlic
1 tablespoon olive oil
1/2 cup dry red wine
1 tablespoon sugar
2 tablespoons Italian seasoning

1/2 teaspoon black pepper
1/4 teaspoon crushed red pepper
2 (28-ounce) cans crushed tomatoes
2 (28-ounce) cans diced tomatoes
2 (6-ounce) cans tomato paste
Hot cooked pasta

Sauté the onions and garlic in the hot olive oil in a Dutch oven over medium heat until the onions are golden brown. Stir in the wine. Cook for 3 to 5 minutes, stirring occasionally. Add the sugar, Italian seasoning, black pepper, red pepper, undrained crushed tomatoes, undrained diced tomatoes and tomato paste and mix well. Bring to a boil and reduce the heat. Simmer for 3 hours, stirring occasionally. Serve over hot cooked pasta. **Makes 9 cups.**

Contributed by Jackie Ludwig

Roasted Red Pepper Sauce

5 tablespoons butter
3 tablespoons all-purpose flour
1 cup heavy cream
1 1/2 teaspoons Beau Monde seasoning
1 tablespoon Italian seasoning

1/4 cup pinot grigio
1/2 (8-ounce) jar roasted red
   peppers, chopped
Hot cooked pasta

Melt the butter in a medium saucepan over low heat. Add the flour 1 tablespoon at a time, blending well after each addition and being careful not to brown. Remove from the heat and stir in the cream. Return to the heat. Stir in the Beau Monde seasoning, Italian seasoning and wine. Cook for 5 minutes. Stir in the roasted red peppers. Serve over hot cooked pasta. **Serves 4.**

Contributed by Rochelle McAvoy

Pasta with Sun-Dried Tomato Cream Sauce

4 large garlic cloves, finely chopped
1 tablespoon olive oil
1 cup chopped drained oil-pack sun-dried tomatoes
1 cup whipping cream
1 (7-ounce) jar roasted red peppers, drained and chopped
1/2 teaspoon crushed red pepper
1 cup chopped fresh basil leaves
8 ounces penne
Salt to taste
16 ounces Parmesan cheese, grated
Pepper to taste

Sauté the garlic in the olive oil in a skillet for 1 minute. Add the sun-dried tomatoes, cream, roasted red peppers and crushed red pepper and mix well. Simmer over medium heat for 2 minutes. Stir in 1/2 cup of the basil and simmer for 1 minute.

Cook the pasta in boiling salted water in a large saucepan until tender but still firm to the bite, stirring occasionally. Drain the pasta, reserving 3/4 cup of the liquid. Return the pasta to the saucepan. Add the sauce, Parmesan cheese and remaining 1/2 cup basil and toss to coat. Add enough of the reserved cooking liquid to moisten if needed. Season with salt and pepper. **Serves 4 to 6.**

Contributed by Lisa Joubert

Pasta with Sausage and Tomato Cream Sauce

16 ounces pasta, such as bow tie, rigatoni or penne
1 pound sweet Italian sausage, casings removed
1/2 teaspoon red pepper flakes
2 tablespoons olive oil
1 onion, chopped
3 garlic cloves, minced
1 (28-ounce) can plum tomatoes, drained and chopped
1 cup whipping cream
Dash of salt
Freshly grated Parmesan cheese
Chopped fresh parsley

Cook the pasta using the package directions; drain. Brown the sausage with the red pepper flakes in the olive oil in a large skillet, stirring until the sausage is crumbly. Add the onion and garlic and cook for 5 minutes. Add the tomatoes, cream and salt. Simmer for 10 minutes or until thickened, stirring frequently. Spoon over the pasta and sprinkle with Parmesan cheese and parsley. **Serves 4 to 6.**

Contributed by Karen Johnston-Gentry

Baked Spaghetti

1 pound ground beef or ground turkey
1 cup chopped onion
1 cup chopped green bell pepper
1 tablespoon butter
1 (28-ounce) can chopped tomatoes
1 (4-ounce) can mushrooms, drained
1 (2-ounce) can sliced black
   olives, drained
2 teaspoons oregano

12 ounces spaghetti, cooked
   and drained
2 cups (8 ounces) shredded
   Cheddar cheese
1 (10-ounce) can cream of
   mushroom soup
1/4 cup water
1/4 cup (1 ounce) grated
   Parmesan cheese

Brown the ground beef in a skillet, stirring until crumbly; drain. Sauté the onion and bell pepper in the butter in a large skillet until tender. Add the undrained tomatoes, mushrooms, olives and oregano and mix well. Stir in the ground beef and simmer for 10 minutes. Place one-half of the spaghetti in a greased 9×13-inch baking dish. Spread one-half of the ground beef mixture over the spaghetti layer and sprinkle with 1 cup of the Cheddar cheese. Repeat the layers with the remaining spaghetti, ground beef mixture and Cheddar cheese. Mix the soup and water in a bowl until smooth. Pour over the layers. Sprinkle with the Parmesan cheese. Bake at 350 degrees for 30 to 35 minutes or until heated through. For extra flavor, use zesty diced tomatoes with jalapeño chiles and Pepper Jack cheese with jalapeño chiles. **Serves 6 to 8.**

Contributed by Lisa Joubert

Overnight Lasagna

1 pound ground beef
1 (32-ounce) jar pasta sauce
15 ounces cottage cheese
1 egg
2 tablespoons chives
1/2 teaspoon oregano
16 ounces lasagna noodles
16 ounces mozzarella cheese, shredded

Brown the ground beef in a skillet, stirring until crumbly; drain. Add the pasta sauce and mix well. Mix the cottage cheese, egg, chives and oregano in a bowl. Alternate layers of the ground beef mixture, lasagna noodles, cottage cheese mixture and mozzarella cheese in a large baking dish until all of the ingredients are used. Chill, covered, for 8 to 10 hours. Uncover and bake at 350 degrees for 50 to 60 minutes or until cooked through. **Serves 6 to 8.**

Contributed by Missie Rolinitis

The miracle is this—the more we share, the more we have. —Leonard Nimoy

Sour Cream Apple Chicken

4 boneless skinless chicken breasts
1 tablespoon vegetable oil
2 baking apples, peeled and thinly sliced
$1/2$ cup apple juice or cider
$1/3$ cup chopped onion
1 teaspoon dried basil
$1/2$ teaspoon salt
1 cup sour cream
1 tablespoon all-purpose flour
4 cups cooked spinach noodles

Cook the chicken in the oil in a large skillet over medium heat for 6 to 8 minutes on each side or until cooked through. Remove from the skillet and keep warm. Add the apples, apple juice, onion, basil and salt to the drippings in the skillet. Bring to a boil and reduce the heat. Simmer until the apples are tender. Mix the sour cream and flour in a bowl. Stir into the apple mixture. Cook until the apple sauce is warm; do not boil. Arrange the noodles on a serving platter and top with the chicken. Spoon the apple sauce over the top. **Serves 4.**

Contributed by Gina Shell-LaMore

Chicken Tetrazzini

8 ounces noodles, cooked and drained
3 tablespoons butter
1/4 cup all-purpose flour
1 teaspoon salt
1/2 teaspoon celery salt
1/2 teaspoon paprika
2 cups milk
1 cup chicken broth
3 cups chopped cooked chicken
3/4 cup (3 ounces) grated Parmesan cheese

Toss the hot cooked pasta with 1 tablespoon of the butter in a bowl to coat. Melt the remaining 2 tablespoons butter in a skillet. Blend in the flour, salt, celery salt and paprika. Cook over low heat until smooth, stirring constantly. Remove from the heat. Stir in the milk and broth. Bring to a boil, stirring constantly. Boil for 1 minute, stirring constantly. Add the chicken, pasta and 1/4 cup of the Parmesan cheese and cook until heated through. Spoon into a baking dish and sprinkle with the remaining 1/2 cup Parmesan cheese. Bake at 350 degrees for 30 minutes. You may add sliced mushrooms, if desired, when you add the chicken. **Serves 8.**

Contributed by Krista Borschnack

Halibut Lasagna

2 tablespoons butter or margarine
1 1/2 pounds halibut steaks, bones
    removed and fish cut into
    1-inch pieces
2 garlic cloves, minced
3/4 teaspoon dried thyme
1/4 cup (1/2 stick) butter or margarine
1/3 cup all-purpose flour

1/2 teaspoon salt
1 1/2 cups chicken broth
1 cup whipping cream
8 ounces lasagna noodles, cooked
    and drained
2 cups (8 ounces) shredded
    Swiss cheese
Minced fresh parsley (optional)

Melt 2 tablespoons butter in a large skillet over medium heat. Add the fish, garlic and thyme. Cook for 10 minutes or until the fish flakes easily with a fork. Remove the fish and set aside. Add 1/4 cup butter to the drippings in the skillet. Stir in the flour and salt until smooth. Cook until golden brown, stirring constantly. Add the broth and cream gradually, stirring constantly. Bring to a boil and cook for 2 minutes or until thickened, stirring constantly.

Layer the noodles, fish, sauce and cheese one-half at a time in a greased 9×13-inch baking dish. Cover and bake at 350 degrees for 20 minutes. Uncover and bake for 20 minutes longer or until bubbly. Let stand for 15 minutes. Sprinkle with parsley before serving. **Serves 6.**

Contributed by Sherri Crawford

Pasta with Salmon, Spinach and Tomatoes

16 ounces bow tie pasta
1/2 cup chicken broth
1 pound salmon, cooked, bones removed and
    salmon broken into chunks
8 ounces cream cheese, cut into cubes
1 (10-ounce) package frozen chopped spinach,
    thawed and drained
1 teaspoon minced garlic
1 teaspoon salt
1 teaspoon pepper
1 tablespoon lemon juice
15 cherry tomatoes, cut into halves
1/2 cup (2 ounces) grated Parmesan cheese

Cook the pasta using the package directions; drain. Heat one-half of the broth and
the salmon in a large skillet. Add the cream cheese and cook until the cream cheese
melts, stirring frequently. Add the remaining broth, the spinach, garlic, salt, pepper
and lemon juice. Cook for 3 to 5 minutes or until combined. Add the cherry
tomatoes and cook for 2 minutes or until softened. Add the hot cooked pasta and
toss to coat. Spoon into a serving bowl and sprinkle with the Parmesan cheese.
You may use cream cheese with 1/3 less fat. **Serves 6.**

A great way to get your kids to eat spinach and salmon.

Contributed by Ann O'Gorman

First-Date Linguini and Clam Sauce

2 (6-ounce) cans clams
5 garlic cloves, minced
1/4 cup olive oil
16 ounces linguini, cooked and drained
2 teaspoons dried parsley
5 teaspoons grated Romano cheese

Drain the clams, reserving one-half of the clam liquid. Sauté the garlic in the olive oil in a shallow skillet until translucent, being careful not to burn. Add the reserved clam liquid and cook for 2 minutes. Stir in the clams. Cook for 1 minute or until warm. Do not overcook. Pour over the hot cooked pasta in a bowl and toss to coat. Sprinkle with the parsley and cheese. Serve with asparagus spears on the side. **Serves 2.**

Contributed by Kim Donald

It's easy to make a buck. It's a lot tougher to make a difference. —Tom Brokaw

Shrimp and Roma Tomatoes with Pasta

1 (12-ounce) package frozen
    shrimp, peeled and deveined
9 ounces refrigerated spinach
    fettuccini or plain fettuccini
1 onion, chopped
1 teaspoon minced garlic
1 tablespoon olive oil
4 Roma tomatoes, chopped
2 teaspoons tarragon
1/4 teaspoon pepper

Cook the shrimp with the pasta in a large saucepan using the package directions for
the pasta. Drain and return to the hot saucepan. Sauté the onion and garlic in the
hot olive oil in a medium saucepan until the onion is tender. Stir in the tomatoes,
tarragon and pepper. Cook over low heat for 2 to 3 minutes or until heated through,
stirring constantly. Add to the pasta mixture and toss to coat. **Serves 4.**

Contributed by Gina Shell-LaMore

Vegetables and Side Dishes

Kankakee Depot, home of the Kankakee Railroad Museum

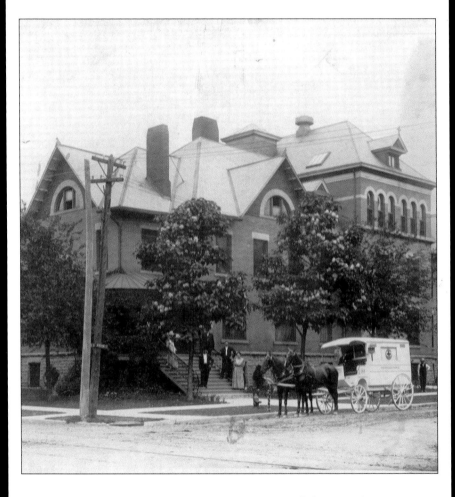

Kankakee Emergency Hospital located at
North 5th Avenue and Merchant Street

Boston Baked Beans

1 onion, chopped
1 tablespoon butter
3 (20- to 24-ounce) cans vegetarian beans
1/4 cup packed dark brown sugar
2 tablespoons mustard
3/4 teaspoon allspice

Sauté the onion in the butter in a skillet until tender. Combine the beans, sautéed onion, brown sugar, mustard and allspice in a large bowl and mix well. Spoon into a large baking dish and bake at 350 degrees for 2 hours. You may need to bake longer if you use a deep baking dish or less if you use a shallow baking dish. **Serves 8.**

Contributed by Allison Beasley

There is one thing more exasperating than a wife who can cook and won't and that's a wife who can't cook and will. —Robert Frost

Deluxe Vegetarian Baked Beans

1 onion, chopped
2 packages ground soy product
1 (15-ounce) can butter beans
1 (15-ounce) can kidney beans
1 (15-ounce) can Great Northern beans
1 (20- to 24-ounce) can vegetarian beans
1 1/4 cups ketchup
3/4 cup packed brown sugar
2 or 3 dashes Worcestershire sauce

Sauté the onion and soy product in a nonstick skillet until the onion is translucent. Combine with the beans, ketchup, brown sugar and Worcestershire sauce in a large bowl and mix well. Spoon into a 3-quart baking dish. Bake at 350 degrees for 45 minutes. **Serves 16 to 20.**

Contributed by Debi Baron

I've seen and met angels wearing the disguise of ordinary people living ordinary lives.
—Tracy Chapman

Balsamic Green Beans

1¹/2 pounds green beans, trimmed and
    cut into 1¹/2-inch pieces
¹/2 cup olive oil
3 tablespoons balsamic vinegar
¹/2 teaspoon Dijon mustard
1 garlic clove, minced (optional)
1 small onion, finely chopped
Pepper to taste
¹/2 cup (2 ounces) shredded Parmesan cheese

Steam the green beans in a steamer until tender-crisp. Plunge immediately into ice water in a bowl to stop the cooking process; drain and pat dry. Place the green beans in a serving bowl. Whisk the olive oil, vinegar, Dijon mustard and garlic in a small bowl. Stir in the onion and pepper. Pour over the green beans and toss to coat. Serve at room temperature or chill, covered, in the refrigerator until ready to serve. Add the cheese and toss to coat just before serving. **Serves 8.**

Contributed by Kerri Lilienthal

Haricots Verts with Pecans and Lemons

1/2 cup pecans
1 pound green beans, trimmed
Salt to taste
3 tablespoons sherry vinegar
1 teaspoon sugar
1/4 teaspoon salt
Freshly ground pepper to taste
1/4 cup olive oil
1 teaspoon freshly grated lemon zest

Spread the pecans in a single layer on a rimmed baking sheet. Bake at 425 degrees for 5 minutes or until toasted. Cool the pecans and coarsely chop.

Cook the green beans in boiling salted water in a saucepan for 3 to 4 minutes or until bright green and tender-crisp; drain. Place in a serving dish and add the pecans.

Whisk the vinegar, sugar, 1/4 teaspoon salt and pepper in a small bowl. Add the olive oil in a slow steady stream, whisking constantly until emulsified. Pour over the green bean mixture and toss to coat. Sprinkle with the lemon zest. **Serves 6.**

Contributed by Melissa Fischer

Oven-Roasted Cauliflower

1 head cauliflower
1 red onion, thinly sliced
3 garlic cloves, minced
1/3 cup olive oil
1 teaspoon thyme
Salt and pepper to taste
1/3 cup grated Parmesan cheese

Break the cauliflower into small pieces and place in a large bowl. Add the onion and garlic. Drizzle the olive oil over the top and toss to coat. Spread in a single layer in a 9×13-inch baking dish. Roast at 400 degrees for 45 minutes, shaking the pan every 15 minutes. Sprinkle with the thyme, salt, pepper and cheese just before serving. **Serves 6.**

Contributed by Karen Johnston-Gentry

We often take for granted the very things that most deserve our gratitude. —Cynthia Ozick

New Orleans Corn Pudding

6 tablespoons butter
2 tablespoons granulated sugar
2 tablespoons (scant) all-purpose flour
1/2 cup heavy cream
4 eggs, well beaten
1 1/2 teaspoons baking powder
2 (16-ounce) packages frozen whole kernel
    yellow or white corn
2 tablespoons butter, melted
2 tablespoons brown sugar
1/4 teaspoon cinnamon

Melt 6 tablespoons butter with the granulated sugar in a saucepan, stirring frequently.
Stir in the flour until blended and remove from the heat. Stir in the cream gradually.
Add the eggs and baking powder and mix well. Stir in the corn. Spoon into a buttered
1 1/2-quart baking dish or soufflé dish. Bake at 350 degrees for 1 hour or until a
knife inserted in the center comes out clean. Spread the top with 2 tablespoons
butter. Sprinkle with a mixture of the brown sugar and cinnamon. Bake for
5 minutes longer. **Serves 12 to 16.**

Contributed by Debi Baron

Corn Soufflé

1 (15-ounce) can yellow whole
    kernel corn
1 (15-ounce) can cream-style corn
1 (8-ounce) package corn bread mix

2 eggs
$^1/_2$ cup (1 stick) butter, sliced
1 cup sour cream
Grated Cheddar cheese

Combine the whole kernel corn, cream-style corn, corn bread mix, eggs, butter and sour cream in a large bowl and mix well. Spoon into a buttered square 2-quart baking dish. Bake at 350 degrees for 1 hour or until light brown. Sprinkle the top with cheese and bake until the cheese melts. **Serves 8.**

Contributed by Mary Burgner

Marinated Cucumbers

6 cucumbers
1 onion, chopped
1 tablespoon white vinegar

$2^1/_2$ teaspoons olive oil
Garlic powder to taste
Salt and pepper to taste

Cut the cucumbers into thin slices and place in a bowl. Add the onion, vinegar, olive oil, garlic powder, salt and pepper and stir to mix well. Cover and marinate in the refrigerator for at least 2 hours before serving. **Serves 6.**

Contributed by Sarah Winkel

Cheesy Potato Bake

1 (2-pound) package frozen Southern-
    style hash brown potatoes, thawed
1 cup fat-free sour cream
1 (10-ounce) can cream of
    chicken soup

4 cups (16 ounces) shredded
    mozzarella cheese
1/2 teaspoon salt
1/2 teaspoon pepper
2 cups crushed cornflakes
1/4 cup (1/2 stick) butter, melted

Mix the potatoes, sour cream, soup, cheese, salt and pepper in a large bowl. Spread
in a 9×13-inch baking dish. Mix the crushed cornflakes and butter in a bowl.
Sprinkle over the potato mixture. Bake at 350 degrees for 1 hour. **Serves 8 to 10.**

Contributed by Melissa Fischer

Cheesy Potatoes

1 (2-pound) package frozen Southern-
    style hash brown potatoes
1/2 cup (1 stick) butter or margarine
8 ounces Velveeta cheese, cut into cubes

1/2 cup (2 ounces) shredded
    Cheddar cheese
2 cups (1 pint) half-and-half

Spread the frozen potatoes in an 11×14-inch baking pan sprayed with nonstick
cooking spray. Combine the butter, Velveeta cheese, Cheddar cheese and half-and-
half in a saucepan and mix well. Cook until melted, stirring constantly. Pour over
the potatoes. Bake at 350 degrees for 1 hour. **Serves 8 to 10.**

Contributed by Kathy Kinmonth

Garlic Mashed Potatoes

5 pounds potatoes
1 garlic bulb
1 teaspoon olive oil
1/2 cup (1 stick) butter, softened
8 ounces cream cheese, softened
1 cup sour cream
2 teaspoons salt
1 teaspoon black pepper
1/8 teaspoon red pepper

Scrub the potatoes and cut into halves or quarters. Boil the potatoes in water to cover in a saucepan until tender; drain. Peel the garlic bulb and cut the cloves horizontally into halves. Place in a small baking dish and drizzle with the olive oil. Bake at 350 degrees for 15 to 20 minutes or until the garlic is soft. Remove from the oven and maintain the oven temperature.

Drain the potatoes and place in a mixing bowl. Add the garlic and mash well. Add the butter, cream cheese, sour cream, salt, black pepper and red pepper and beat well. Spoon into a 9×13-inch baking dish. Bake for 50 to 60 minutes or until light brown. You may peel the potatoes, if desired. **Serves 8 to 10.**

Contributed by Arlene Moore

German Potato Salad

1¹/2 to 2 pounds sliced bacon
3¹/2 pounds potatoes, boiled and peeled
1¹/2 cups chopped onions
¹/4 cup all-purpose flour
¹/4 cup sugar
1¹/2 cups water
¹/4 cup cider vinegar
1¹/2 teaspoons salt
¹/4 teaspoon pepper
¹/2 cup light cream

Cook the bacon in a large skillet until crisp. Drain, reserving 3 tablespoons of the bacon drippings. Crumble the bacon. Cut the potatoes into large pieces. Combine the potatoes, onions, bacon and reserved bacon drippings in a large bowl and toss to mix. Mix the flour, sugar, water, vinegar, salt and pepper in a skillet until blended. Cook until thickened and bubbly, stirring constantly. Stir in the cream. Pour over the potato mixture and toss gently to coat. Serve warm. **Serves 6.**

Contributed by Sarah Bowman-Steffes

Herbed New Potatoes

12 small new potatoes
1/4 cup (1/2 stick) butter
4 teaspoons minced fresh parsley,
    or 1 1/2 teaspoons dried parsley
4 teaspoons minced fresh chives,
    or 1 1/3 teaspoons dried chives

Peel a 1/2-inch strip around the center of each potato and immediately place in cold water in a medium saucepan. Add enough additional water to cover by 2 inches. Bring to a boil over medium-high heat. Boil for 20 minutes or until the potatoes can be pierced easily with a fork but are still firm; drain and keep warm.

Microwave the butter in a microwave-safe bowl on High until melted. Stir in the parsley and chives. Pour over the potatoes and toss to coat. Spoon into a serving bowl and serve immediately. **Serves 6.**

Contributed by Lesley Robinson

Make-Ahead Potatoes

12 large potatoes, peeled and boiled
8 ounces cream cheese, softened
1 cup sour cream
1 teaspoon onion powder or salt
$^1/_2$ teaspoon garlic salt
$^1/_4$ cup ($^1/_2$ stick) butter, melted
Paprika to taste

Combine the cooked potatoes, cream cheese, sour cream, onion powder and garlic salt in a large bowl and whip or mash until fluffy, adding milk if needed to reach the desired consistency. Spread in a buttered 9×13-inch baking dish and chill or freeze until ready to serve. To serve, spread the top with the melted butter and sprinkle with paprika. Bake at 325 degrees for 45 minutes. Increase the baking temperature to 350 degrees if you use a baking pan instead of a baking dish. Serves 4 to 6.

Contributed by Christine Betts

Sweet Potato Casserole

4 cups mashed baked sweet potatoes
1/2 cup granulated sugar
2 eggs
1/4 cup (1/2 stick) butter, softened
1 cup milk
1/2 teaspoon nutmeg
1/2 teaspoon cinnamon
1/4 cup (1/2 stick) butter, melted
1/2 cup packed brown sugar
3/4 cup crushed cornflakes
1/2 cup chopped pecans

Combine the sweet potatoes, granulated sugar, eggs, 1/4 cup butter, the milk, nutmeg and cinnamon in a bowl and mix well. Spoon into a baking dish. Bake at 400 degrees for 25 minutes. Mix 1/4 cup melted butter, the brown sugar, cornflakes and pecans in a bowl. Spread over the top of the sweet potato mixture and bake for 15 minutes. You may used canned sweet potatoes and reduce the milk to 1/2 cup.
Serves 8.

Contributed by Ann O'Gorman

Roasted Zucchini and Feta Cheese

6 zucchini
Vegetable oil
Garlic pepper to taste
Crumbled feta cheese

Cut the zucchini into slices 3/4 inch wide. Cut each slice into quarters. Spread the zucchini on a baking sheet. Drizzle with oil and sprinkle with garlic pepper. Bake at 400 degrees for 20 minutes. Place in a serving dish and top with feta cheese. **Serves 6.**

Contributed by Sherri Crawford

Volunteers do not necessaarily have the time; they just have the heart. —Elizabeth Andrew

Zucchini Casserole

1 cup baking mix
1/2 cup vegetable oil
4 eggs, beaten
2 tablespoons chopped parsley
1/2 teaspoon seasoned salt
1/2 teaspoon salt
Dash of pepper
4 cups sliced zucchini
1/2 cup chopped onion
1/2 cup (2 ounces) grated Parmesan cheese
1 cup (4 ounces) shredded mozzarella cheese

Combine the baking mix, oil, eggs, parsley, seasoned salt, salt and pepper in a large bowl and mix well. Add the zucchini, onion, Parmesan cheese, and mozzarella cheese and mix well. Spread in a greased 9×13-inch baking dish. Bake at 350 degrees for 30 minutes or until light brown. **Serves 8 to 10.**

Contributed by Leslie Geoffrey

Baked Pineapple

2 cups sugar
1 cup (2 sticks) margarine, melted
3 eggs
1/2 cup evaporated milk
1 teaspoon vanilla extract
4 cups cubed bread
1 (20-ounce) can crushed pineapple, drained

Mix the sugar and margarine in a bowl. Beat the eggs, evaporated milk and vanilla in a bowl until blended. Stir in the bread and pineapple. Add the sugar mixture and mix well. Spoon into a 2-quart baking dish. Bake at 325 degrees for 50 to 60 minutes or until set. **Serves 6.**

Contributed by Jackie Ludwig

Cakes and Pies

The Bradley House, Frank Lloyd Wright, architect

Building at St. Viators

FoxMore Apple Cake

1/2 cup sugar
1 teaspoon cinnamon
3 cups all-purpose flour
1 tablespoon baking powder
1 cup sugar
1/3 cup orange juice
2 1/2 teaspoons vanilla extract
4 eggs
1 cup vegetable oil
3 apples

Mix 1/2 cup sugar and the cinnamon in a small bowl and set aside. Mix the flour, baking powder and 1 cup sugar in a large bowl and make a well in the center. Pour the orange juice, vanilla, eggs and oil into the well in the flour mixture and mix until smooth.

Core and peel the apples. Cut the apples into thin slices. Layer the batter, apples and cinnamon-sugar mixture one-third at a time in a greased and floured tube pan. Bake at 350 degrees for 1 1/4 hours. **Serves 8.**

Contributed by Arlene Moore

Carrot Cake with Cream Cheese Frosting

CAKE
2 cups all-purpose flour
1 tablespoon cinnamon
2 teaspoons baking soda
1 teaspoon salt
4 eggs
2 cups sugar
1 1/2 cups vegetable oil
3 cups grated carrots
1 cup nuts
1 cup raisins
1 cup shredded coconut (optional)
2 teaspoons vanilla extract

CREAM CHEESE FROSTING
8 ounces cream cheese, softened
1/2 cup (1 stick) butter, softened
1 teaspoon vanilla extract
1 (16-ounce) package
    confectioners' sugar

To prepare the cake, mix the flour, cinnamon, baking soda and salt together. Beat the eggs, sugar and oil in a mixing bowl until blended. Add the flour mixture and mix well. Stir in the carrots, nuts, raisins, coconut and vanilla. Pour into two greased and floured 8-inch cake pans. Bake at 350 degrees for 1 hour or until the layers test done. Cool in the pans on wire racks for 10 minutes. Invert onto wire racks to cool.

To prepare the frosting, beat the cream cheese, butter and vanilla in a mixing bowl until light and fluffy. Add the confectioners' sugar and beat until smooth. Spread between the layers and over the top and side of the cake. **Serves 10.**

This is a very moist cake. For variation, spread apricot preserves between the cake layers before frosting the top and side of the cake.

Contributed by Bernadette Henriott

Cherry Dump Cake

1 (21-ounce) can cherry pie filling
1 (21-ounce) can crushed pineapple
1 (2-layer) package white or yellow
    cake mix

1 cup (2 sticks) butter or
    margarine, melted
1 cup pecans, chopped

Layer the pie filling, undrained pineapple, cake mix, butter and pecans in the order listed in a 10×14-inch cake pan. Do not mix. Bake at 350 degrees for 55 minutes. Cool before serving. **Serves 12 to 16.**

Contributed by Katie Reed

Cherry Chocolate Cake

1 (2-layer) package chocolate cake mix
1/4 teaspoon baking soda
1/3 cup boiling water
2 eggs

1 teaspoon cherry extract or almond
    extract (optional)
1 (21-ounce) can cherry pie filling

Combine the cake mix, baking soda, water, eggs and cherry extract in a mixing bowl. Beat for 2 minutes or until light and fluffy. Fold in the pie filling. Pour into a greased 9×13-inch cake pan. Bake at 350 degrees for 35 to 45 minutes or until the cake tests done. **Serves 12.**

Bake 1 or 2 days ahead for enhanced flavor.

Contributed by Bernadette Henroitt

Molten Chocolate Cakes

1¹/4 cups (2¹/2 sticks) butter
³/4 cup semisweet chocolate chips
4 eggs
¹/2 cup sugar

³/4 cup all-purpose flour
12 caramel candies
¹/4 cup evaporated milk
Confectioners' sugar

Melt the butter and chocolate chips in a saucepan, stirring constantly. Remove from the heat to cool slightly. Beat the eggs and sugar at medium speed in a large mixing bowl for 5 minutes or until thick. Add the flour gradually, beating constantly at low speed. Add the chocolate mixture and beat for 3 minutes. Fill greased muffin cups two-thirds full. Bake at 325 degrees for 5 minutes.

Unwrap the caramels. Heat the caramels and 2 tablespoons of the evaporated milk in a saucepan until melted, stirring constantly. Spoon 2 teaspoons of the caramel mixture over the cake in each muffin cup. Bake for 8 minutes. Remove from the oven and cool for a few minutes. Invert the cakes onto individual serving plates. Mix the remaining caramel mixture and the remaining 2 tablespoons evaporated milk in a bowl and stir to mix well. Serve over the warm cakes. Sprinkle with confectioners' sugar. **Serves 10.**

Contributed by Sherri Crawford

Milky Way Cake by Sister Patsy

1/2 cup (1 stick) margarine
8 to 10 small Milky Way candy bars
1/2 cup (1 stick) margarine, softened
2 cups sugar
4 eggs
1 teaspoon vanilla extract
2 1/2 cups all-purpose flour
1 3/4 cups buttermilk
1/2 teaspoon baking soda

Melt 1/2 cup margarine in a saucepan over low heat. Add the candy bars and heat until melted, stirring constantly. Beat 1/2 cup margarine and the sugar in a mixing bowl until light and fluffy. Add the eggs, vanilla, flour, buttermilk and baking soda and mix well. Stir in the melted candy mixture. Pour into a nonstick bundt pan and bake at 350 degrees for 60 to 70 minutes or until the cake tests done. Cool in the pan for 10 minutes. Invert onto a wire rack to cool completely. **Serves 8 to 10.**

This cake may be baked in two nonstick 5×9-inch loaf pans for 1 hour or until the loaves test done.

Contributed by Sarah Bowman-Steffes

Delicious Delores Cake

2¼ cups all-purpose flour
2 teaspoons baking soda
1 teaspoon salt
1 (16-ounce) can fruit cocktail
¼ cup (½ stick) butter, softened
2 eggs
1 cup packed brown sugar
2 cups (12 ounces) semisweet chocolate chips

Mix the flour, baking soda and salt together. Combine the fruit cocktail, butter, eggs and brown sugar in a bowl and mix well. Add the flour mixture and beat at medium speed for 2 minutes. Stir in the chocolate chips. Pour into a greased and floured 9×13-inch cake pan. Bake at 350 degrees for 35 to 40 minutes or until the cake tests done. **Serves 12.**

It may sound odd, but this cake is very moist and delicious.

Contributed by Ann O'Gorman

Chocolate Oatmeal Cake

1³/4 cups all-purpose flour
1 teaspoon baking soda
¹/2 teaspoon salt
1 tablespoon baking cocoa
1³/4 cups boiling water
1 cup quick-cooking oats
1 cup packed brown sugar
1 cup granulated sugar
1 cup (2 sticks) butter, softened
2 eggs, lightly beaten
1 teaspoon vanilla extract
2 cups (12 ounces) semisweet chocolate chips

Mix the flour, baking soda, salt and baking cocoa together and set aside. Pour
the boiling water over the oats in a large bowl and let stand for 10 minutes.
Add the brown sugar, granulated sugar and butter and stir until the butter melts.
Add the eggs and vanilla and mix well. Add the flour mixture and mix well.
Stir in 1 cup of the chocolate chips. Pour into a greased 9×13-inch cake pan. Sprinkle
the remaining chocolate chips over the top. Bake at 350 degrees for 40 minutes.
Serves 12.

Contributed by Karen Johnston-Gentry

Pig Licking Cake

1 (2-layer) package yellow cake mix
3/4 cup vegetable oil
4 eggs
1 (11-ounce) can mandarin oranges, drained
1 (4-ounce) package vanilla instant pudding mix
1 medium can crushed pineapple, drained
8 ounces cream cheese, softened
8 ounces whipped topping

Combine the cake mix, oil, eggs and mandarin oranges in a large bowl and mix well. Pour into a greased and floured 9×13-inch cake pan. Bake at 325 degrees for 35 to 40 minutes or until the cake tests done. Remove from the oven to cool.

Mix the pudding mix and pineapple in a bowl. Add the cream cheese and whipped topping and mix well. Spread over the cooled cake. **Serves 16 to 20.**

Contributed by Katie Reed

Wine makes a symphony of a good meal. —Fernande Garvin (The Art of French Cooking)

Pistachio Pudding Cake

2 (4-ounce) packages pistachio pudding mix
1 (2-layer) package white cake mix
1/2 cup milk
1/2 cup water
1/2 cup vegetable oil
5 eggs
1/2 cup nuts (optional)

Combine the pudding mix, cake mix, milk, water, oil, eggs and nuts in a large mixing bowl and mix until blended. Pour into a greased and floured bundt pan. Bake at 350 degrees for 45 minutes or until a wooden pick inserted in the center comes out clean. Cool in the pan for 10 minutes. Invert onto a wire rack to cool completely. **Serves 12.**

This cake is the consistency of pound cake. Changing the flavor of the pudding mix varies the cake. Try using lemon or other flavors of pudding mix for variety.

Contributed by Jane Koehler

Fast Pound Cake

1 (2-layer) package yellow cake mix
8 ounces cream cheese, softened
4 eggs
1/2 cup water

Combine the cake mix, cream cheese, eggs and water in a mixing bowl and mix well. Pour into a greased bundt pan or 10-inch tube pan. Bake at 350 degrees for 40 minutes or until the cake tests done. Cool in the pan for 10 minutes. Invert onto a wire rack to cool completely. **Serves 12.**

This makes a good strawberry shortcake.

Contributed by Bernadette Henriott

Fall Pumpkin Cake Bars

CAKE
2 cups all-purpose flour
1/2 teaspoon baking powder
1 teaspoon baking soda
2 teaspoons cinnamon
4 eggs
1 cup vegetable oil
2 cups sugar
1/2 cup canned pumpkin
1 cup nuts

CREAM CHEESE FROSTING
3 ounces cream cheese, softened
6 tablespoons butter, softened
1 teaspoon vanilla extract
1 teaspoon milk
3/4 cup confectioners' sugar

To prepare the cake, mix the flour, baking powder, baking soda and cinnamon together. Beat the eggs, oil, sugar and pumpkin in a mixing bowl. Add the flour mixture and mix thoroughly. Stir in the nuts. Pour into a greased and floured 12×18-inch cake pan. Bake at 350 degrees for 20 to 25 minutes or until the cake tests done. Remove from the oven and cool slightly.

To prepare the frosting, combine the cream cheese, butter, vanilla and milk in a mixing bowl and beat well. Add the confectioners' sugar and beat until smooth. Spread over the warm cake and cut into bars. **Serves 10 to 12.**

Contributed by Arlene Moore

Rum Cake

CAKE
1 (2-layer) package yellow cake mix
1 (4-ounce) package vanilla instant pudding mix
4 eggs
1/2 cup canola oil
1 cup dark rum

RUM GLAZE
1/2 cup (1 stick) butter or margarine
1/4 cup water
1 cup sugar
1/2 cup rum

To prepare the cake, combine the cake mix, pudding mix, eggs, oil and rum in a mixing bowl and beat until smooth. Pour into a greased and floured bundt pan or tube pan. Bake at 325 degrees for 1 hour. Cool in the pan for 10 minutes. Invert onto a cake plate to cool completely.

To prepare the glaze, melt the butter in a saucepan. Stir in the water and sugar. Bring to a boil and boil for 5 minutes, stirring constantly. Stir in the rum. Drizzle over the cake. **Serves 12.**

Contributed by Gail Passwater

Ron's Strawberry Dream Cake

1 (2-layer) package butter-recipe cake mix
1 (6-ounce) package strawberry gelatin
2 cups boiling water
1 (4-ounce) package vanilla instant pudding mix
8 ounces whipped topping

Prepare the cake mix and bake using the package directions for a 9×13-inch cake pan. Poke holes in the hot cake with the end of a wooden spoon. Dissolve the gelatin in the boiling water in a bowl. Pour over the cake. Let stand until cool. Prepare the pudding mix using the package directions. Spread over the cooled cake. Top with the whipped topping. **Serves 10.**

Contributed by Allison Beasley

You don't get over hating to cook, anymore than you get over having big feet. —Author unknown

Swedish Apple Pie

5 or 6 large apples, cored, peeled and sliced
1 tablespoon sugar
1 tablespoon cinnamon
1 cup all-purpose flour
1 cup sugar
Pinch of salt
3/4 cup (1 1/2 sticks) butter, melted
1 egg, beaten

Fill a buttered 9-inch pie plate two-thirds full with the apples. Sprinkle with a mixture of 1 tablespoon sugar and the cinnamon. Combine the flour, 1 cup sugar, salt, butter and egg in a bowl and mix well. Pour over the apples. Bake at 350 degrees for 45 minutes or until the crust is golden brown. **Serves 8.**

Delicious and easy to make.

Contributed by Gail Passwater

Coconut Cream Pie

2/3 cup sugar
1/3 cup cornstarch
2 tablespoons all-purpose flour
1/4 teaspoon salt
3 eggs
3 cups milk
1 tablespoon butter
2 teaspoons vanilla extract
1 cup flaked coconut
1 (9-inch) chocolate or graham cracker pie shell

Combine the sugar, cornstarch, flour and salt in a heavy saucepan. Whisk in the eggs until blended. Add the milk gradually, whisking constantly. Bring to a boil over medium heat and boil for 1 minute, whisking constantly. The mixture will appear curdled but will eventually be smooth. Remove from the heat. Add the butter, vanilla and coconut and mix well. Pour into the pie shell and cover with waxed paper. Chill for 4 hours or until set. Serve with whipped topping and toasted coconut. **Serves 8.**

Contributed by Bernadette Henriott

Frozen Peanut Butter Cup Pie

CRUST
1/2 cup all-purpose flour
2 tablespoons brown sugar
1/4 cup pecans, crushed
1/4 cup (1/2 stick) margarine,
    cut into pieces

**PEANUT BUTTER FILLING
AND ASSEMBLY**
1 cup confectioners' sugar
1/2 cup milk
3/4 cup peanut butter
4 ounces cream cheese, softened
8 ounces whipped topping
1 (16-ounce) can chocolate syrup

To prepare the crust, mix the flour, brown sugar and pecans in a bowl. Cut in the margarine until crumbly. Place in a 9-inch pie plate. Bake at 350 degrees for 15 minutes, stirring every few minutes to keep crumbly.

To prepare the filling and assemble, combine the confectioners' sugar, milk, peanut butter and cream cheese in a large mixing bowl and beat until smooth. Fold in the whipped topping. Pour over the crust. Drizzle with the chocolate syrup and run a wooden pick through the syrup to form designs. Freeze for 8 to 10 hours or until firm. **Serves 8 to 10.**

Contributed by Rochelle McAvoy

No one is more cherished in this world than someone who lightens the burden of another.
—Author unknown

Desserts

The Original Dairy Queen was founded in Kankakee.

Arcade Building circa 1890

Chocolate Chip Mocha Cheesecake

2¼ cups graham cracker crumbs
1¼ cups (2½ sticks) butter, melted
2 cups (12 ounces) miniature
    semisweet chocolate chips
1 envelope unflavored gelatin
1 tablespoon instant coffee granules

½ cup milk
2 cups heavy whipping cream, chilled
16 ounces cream cheese, softened
1 (14-ounce) can sweetened
    condensed milk

Mix the graham cracker crumbs and butter in a bowl. Let stand until cool.
Stir in one-half of the chocolate chips. Press over the bottom and up the side of
a springform pan.

Soften the gelatin in a small amount of water in a small saucepan. Stir in the coffee
granules and milk. Heat until the gelatin and coffee granules are dissolved, stirring
frequently. Let stand until cool.

Whip the cream in a mixing bowl until stiff peaks form. Combine the cream cheese,
condensed milk and the coffee mixture in a mixing bowl and beat until smooth.
Add the whipped cream and blend until smooth and creamy. Fold in the remaining
1 cup chocolate chips. Pour into the prepared pan and chill, covered, for 8 to
10 hours. **Serves 6 to 8.**

Contributed by Lisa Joubert

Pumpkin Swirl Cheesecake

25 gingersnaps, finely crushed
 (about 1 1/2 cups)
1/2 cup finely chopped pecans
1/4 cup (1/2 stick) butter, melted
32 ounces cream cheese, softened
3/4 cup sugar
1 teaspoon vanilla extract

4 eggs
1/4 cup sugar
1 cup canned pumpkin
1 teaspoon cinnamon
1/4 teaspoon nutmeg
Dash of cloves

Mix the gingersnap crumbs, pecans and butter in a bowl. Press firmly over the bottom and 1 inch up the side of a 9-inch springform pan.

Beat the cream cheese, 3/4 cup sugar and the vanilla in a mixing bowl until blended. Add the eggs one at a time, beating at low speed after each addition just until blended. Remove 1 1/2 cups of the batter to a small bowl. Stir 1/4 cup sugar, the pumpkin, cinnamon, nutmeg and cloves into the remaining batter. Spoon one-half of the pumpkin batter into the prepared pan. Top with spoonfuls of one-half of the reserved batter. Repeat the layers with the pumpkin batter and remaining reserved batter. Cut through with a knife to marbleize.

Bake at 325 degrees for 55 minutes or until the center is almost set. Remove from the oven to cool completely. Chill, covered, for 4 to 10 hours. Store in the refrigerator. If you use a dark springform pan, reduce the baking temperature to 300 degrees.
Serves 6 to 8.

Contributed by Mary Burgner

Grandma's Blueberry Cobbler

4 cups fresh blueberries
1 teaspoon lemon juice
1 cup all-purpose flour
1/2 cup sugar
1 teaspoon baking powder
1/4 teaspoon nutmeg
Pinch of salt
1 tablespoon vegetable oil
1/2 teaspoon vanilla extract
2 egg whites, lightly beaten
3 tablespoons sugar
1/2 teaspoon cinnamon

Toss the blueberries with the lemon juice in a bowl. Place in a baking dish coated with nonstick cooking spray. Mix the flour, 1/2 cup sugar, the baking powder, nutmeg and salt in a bowl and make a well in the center. Whisk the oil, vanilla and egg whites in a bowl to blend. Pour into the well in the flour mixture and blend until moist. Drop the dough by spoonfuls onto the blueberry mixture to form eight dumplings. Mix 3 tablespoons sugar and the cinnamon together and sprinkle over the dumplings. Bake at 350 degrees for 30 minutes or until the filling is bubbly and the dumplings are light brown. **Serves 8.**

Contributed by Rochelle McAvoy

Dirt Cake Dessert

4 cups milk
1 (4-ounce) package vanilla instant
    pudding mix
8 ounces cream cheese, softened
1/4 cup (1/2 stick) butter, softened
1/2 cup confectioners' sugar
12 ounces whipped topping
1 (16-ounce) package chocolate
    sandwich cookies, finely crushed

Whisk the milk and pudding mix in a bowl until thickened. Beat the cream cheese and butter in a mixing bowl until creamy. Add the confectioners' sugar and beat until smooth. Fold in the whipped topping.

Reserve one-third of the cookie crumbs. Layer the remaining cookie crumbs, pudding and cream cheese mixture one-half at a time in a sterilized clay flowerpot 8 inches tall and 8 inches in diameter. Sprinkle with the reserved cookie crumbs. Chill in the refrigerator until ready to serve. Garnish with gummy worms and an artificial flower. **Serves 4 to 6.**

Contributed by Missie Rolinitis

Chocolate Éclair Dessert

1 (16-ounce) package graham crackers
1 (4-ounce) package chocolate instant pudding mix
1 (4-ounce) package vanilla instant pudding mix
3$\frac{1}{2}$ cups milk
8 ounces whipped topping
1 (16-ounce) can chocolate frosting

Line one-third of the graham crackers in a buttered 9×13-inch dish. Beat the chocolate pudding mix, vanilla pudding mix and milk at medium speed in a medium mixing bowl for 2 minutes. Blend in the whipped topping. Layer the pudding mixture and remaining graham crackers one-half at a time in the prepared dish, ending with the graham crackers. Spread the frosting over the top. Chill for 2 hours before serving. **Serves 6.**

Contributed by Christine Betts

Creamy Mocha Frozen Dessert

2 teaspoons instant coffee granules
1 tablespoon hot water
1 cup crushed chocolate sandwich cookies
1/2 cup pecans
1/4 cup (1/2 stick) butter or margarine, melted
16 ounces cream cheese, softened
1 (14-ounce) can sweetened condensed milk
1/2 cup chocolate syrup
8 ounces whipped topping
1/4 cup pecans

Dissolve the coffee granules in the hot water in a small bowl. Combine the cookie crumbs, 1/2 cup pecans and the butter in a bowl and mix well. Press over the bottom of a 9×13-inch dish.

Beat the cream cheese in a mixing bowl until light and fluffy. Add the coffee mixture, condensed milk and chocolate syrup and blend well. Fold in the whipped topping. Spread in the prepared dish. Sprinkle with 1/4 cup pecans. Cover and freeze until firm. **Serves 24.**

This dessert can be made into a pie by pouring the filling into a 9-inch chocolate cookie crumb pie shell.

Contributed by Gina Shell-LaMore

S'Mores Dessert Squares

40 vanilla wafers
5 tablespoons butter, melted
3 tablespoons sugar
1¼ cups cold milk
1 (4-ounce) package chocolate instant
    pudding mix
24 vanilla wafers

2 cups cold milk
2 (4-ounce) packages white chocolate
    instant pudding mix
1½ cups whipped topping
1½ cups miniature marshmallows
1 cup (6 ounces) semisweet
    chocolate chips

Finely crush 40 vanilla wafers and place in a medium bowl. Add the butter and sugar and mix until blended. Press the mixture firmly over the bottom of a 9×13-inch baking dish. Bake at 350 degrees for 8 minutes or until light brown.

Whisk 1¼ cups milk and the chocolate pudding mix in a bowl until thick and smooth. Spread over the crust and top with 24 vanilla wafers. Whisk 2 cups milk and the white chocolate pudding mix in a large bowl until thick and smooth. Fold in the whipped topping. Spread over the vanilla wafer layer. Chill for 3 hours or until set.

To serve, top the dessert evenly with the marshmallows and chocolate chips. Broil for 1 minute or until the marshmallows are light brown and the chocolate chips melt. Cut into twelve large pieces or twenty-four smaller pieces and serve immediately. Store any leftovers in the refrigerator. **Serves 12 to 24.**

Contributed by Missie Roinitis

Four-Layer Delight

1 cup all-purpose flour
1/2 cup pecans, chopped
1/2 cup (1 stick) margarine, softened
8 ounces cream cheese, softened
1 cup confectioners' sugar
8 ounces whipped topping
2 (4-ounce) packages any flavor
    instant pudding mix
3 cups cold milk

Mix the flour, pecans and margarine in a bowl until crumbly. Press over the bottom of a 9×13-inch baking dish. Bake at 375 degrees for 15 minutes. Remove from the oven to cool completely.

Beat the cream cheese and confectioners' sugar in a mixing bowl until smooth. Add 1 cup of the whipped topping and mix well. Spread over the cooled crust. Whisk the pudding mix and milk in a bowl until smooth and thick. Spread over the cream cheese layer. Spread the remaining whipped topping over the top. **Serves 12 to 16.**

Contributed by Krista Borschnack

Peanut Butter Chocolate Ice Cream Torte

24 peanut butter cookies
1 (16-ounce) can chocolate syrup
1 gallon vanilla ice cream, softened
1 (28-ounce) jar peanut butter, melted
1/2 (12-ounce) package peanut butter cups, cut into quarters

Layer six of the cookies in the bottom of a torte bowl and drizzle with one-fourth of the chocolate syrup. Cover with one-fourth of the ice cream and drizzle with one-fourth of the peanut butter. Sprinkle with one-fourth of the peanut butter cups. Repeat the layers three times with the remaining ingredients. Cover and freeze until firm. Let thaw for 15 minutes before serving. **Serves 8 to 12.**

Contributed by Christine Betts

It's nice to be important, but it's more important to be nice. —Author unknown

Buckeyes

3 pounds confectioners' sugar
2 pounds peanut butter
2 cups (4 sticks) butter, melted
3 tablespoons vanilla extract

4 cups (24 ounces) semisweet
chocolate chips
1/2 bar (or more) paraffin

Combine the confectioners' sugar, peanut butter, butter and vanilla in a large bowl and mix well. Roll into medium-size balls and place on a baking sheet. Store in a cool place.

Melt the chocolate chips and paraffin in a double boiler over hot water, stirring constantly and adding additional shaved paraffin if needed to reach the desired consistency. Remove from the heat. Dip the peanut butter balls into the chocolate using wooden picks. Return to the baking sheet and smooth over the hole from the wooden pick. Let stand until set. Store in airtight containers in a cool place. **Makes approximately 4 dozen.**

Contributed by Gina Shell-LaMore

Fudge

2/3 cup evaporated milk
3/4 cup (1 1/2 sticks) margarine
3 cups sugar
2 cups (12 ounces) semisweet
chocolate chips

1/2 (5- to 7-ounce) jar
marshmallow creme
1 cup walnuts or pecans, chopped
1 teaspoon vanilla extract

Bring the evaporated milk, margarine and sugar to a boil in a heavy saucepan over medium heat. Boil for 5 minutes, stirring constantly. Remove from the heat. Add the chocolate chips and stir until melted. Add the marshmallow creme, walnuts and vanilla and beat well. Pour into a greased 9×13-inch dish. Cool for 1 hour or until set. Cut into squares. **Serves 20 to 24.**

Contributed by Kathy Kinmonth

Magic Cookie Bars

¹/2 cup (1 stick) butter or margarine
1¹/2 cups graham cracker crumbs
1 (14-ounce) can sweetened condensed milk
1 cup (6 ounces) milk chocolate chips
1¹/3 cups (3¹/2 ounces) flaked coconut
1 cup walnuts, chopped

Melt the butter in a 9×13-inch baking pan in a 350-degree oven. Maintain the oven temperature. Sprinkle the graham cracker crumbs over the butter. Pour the condensed milk evenly over the graham cracker crumbs. Layer the chocolate chips, coconut and walnuts over the top and press down firmly with waxed paper. Bake for 25 to 30 minutes or until light brown. Cool and cut into bars. If you use a glass baking dish, reduce the oven temperature to 325 degrees. **Serves 12 to 16.**

Contributed by Kathy Kinmonth

I prefer to regard dessert as I would imagine the perfect woman: subtle, a little bittersweet, not blowsy and extrovert. Delicately made up, not highly rouged. Holding back, not exposing everything and, of course with a flavor that lasts. —Graham Kerr (The Galloping Gourmet, 1960s)

Quickest Pretzel Treats

30 square bite-size pretzels
30 Rollos
30 pecan halves

Arrange the pretzels in a single layer on a baking sheet. Place a piece of the candy on top of each pretzel. Bake at 350 degrees for 2 to 3 minutes or until the candy melts slightly. Place a pecan half on top while still warm. **Serves 8 to 10.**

Contributed by Kim Donald

Special-K Bars

1 cup light corn syrup
1 cup sugar
1 cup chunky peanut butter
6 cups Special-K cereal
1 cup (6 ounces) butterscotch chips
1 cup (6 ounces) semisweet chocolate chips

Bring the corn syrup and sugar to a boil in a heavy saucepan. Remove from the heat and stir in the peanut butter. Add the cereal and mix until well coated. Press over the bottom of a 9×13-inch dish. Let stand to cool. Combine the butterscotch chips and chocolate chips in a microwave-safe bowl. Microwave on Low at 15-second intervals until melted, stirring after each interval. Stir until the mixture is smooth. Pour over the cereal mixture. Cool and cut into bars. **Makes 24 bars.**

This recipe is great for school bake sales or meetings and yummy to bring to someone's house.

Contributed by Sarah Bowman-Steffes

Graham Nut Toffee Squares

12 graham crackers
1 cup (2 sticks) butter or margarine
1 cup packed brown sugar
1¹/2 cups pecans or walnuts, chopped

Separate the graham crackers at the perforations into rectangles. Line the bottom of a 10×15-inch baking pan completely with the graham crackers. Melt the butter with the brown sugar in a heavy saucepan, stirring frequently. Bring to a boil and cook for exactly 3 minutes. Pour over the graham crackers and sprinkle with the pecans. Bake at 350 degrees for 8 to 10 minutes. **Makes 4 dozen.**

Contributed by Missie Rolinitis

Let's kick it up a notch! Bam! —Emeril Lagasse

Fourth of July Caramel Nut Brownies

1 (14-ounce) package caramel candy
1/3 cup evaporated milk
1 (2-layer) package German chocolate cake mix
3/4 cup (1 1/2 sticks) butter, melted
1/3 cup evaporated milk
1 cup (6 ounces) semisweet chocolate chips
1 cup pecans, chopped

Unwrap the caramels. Combine the caramels and 1/3 cup evaporated milk in a microwave-safe dish. Microwave on Low at 15-second intervals until the caramels are melted and smooth, stirring after each interval.

Combine the cake mix, butter and 1/3 cup evaporated milk in a bowl and mix well. Spread one-half of the batter in a greased 9×13-inch baking pan. Bake at 350 degrees for 6 to 8 minutes or until the top begins to set. Remove from the oven. Sprinkle with the chocolate chips and pecans. Drizzle with the melted caramel. Spoon the remaining batter over the top. Bake for 15 minutes longer or until the brownies are firm to the touch. **Serves 8.**

Contributed by Arlene Moore

Pumpkin Brownies

BROWNIES
2 cups all-purpose flour
2 teaspoons baking powder
2 teaspoons baking soda
1 tablespoon cinnamon
1 teaspoon allspice
1/2 teaspoon nutmeg
2 cups sugar
1 cup vegetable oil
4 eggs
1 (16-ounce) can pumpkin

CREAM CHEESE FROSTING
4 ounces cream cheese, softened
1/4 cup (1/2 stick) butter, softened
1 teaspoon milk
1/4 teaspoon salt
1 teaspoon vanilla extract
1 1/4 cups confectioners' sugar

To prepare the brownies, mix the flour, baking powder, baking soda, cinnamon, allspice and nutmeg together. Combine the sugar, oil, eggs and pumpkin in a bowl and mix until blended. Add the flour mixture and mix well. Spread in a greased and floured 10×15-inch baking pan. Bake at 350 degrees for 20 to 25 minutes or until the edges pull from the sides of the pan. Remove from the oven to cool.

To prepare the frosting, beat the cream cheese and butter in a mixing bowl until creamy. Add the milk, salt, vanilla and confectioners' sugar and beat until smooth. Spread over the cooled brownies. Cut into bars. Store in the refrigerator. **Serves 16.**

Contributed by Karen Johnston-Gentry

Amaretto Chunk Cookies

2¹/2 cups all-purpose flour
1 teaspoon baking soda
1 teaspoon baking powder
¹/2 teaspoon salt
1 cup (2 sticks) butter, softened
1 cup packed brown sugar
¹/2 cup granulated sugar
2 eggs
1 tablespoon amaretto
2 teaspoons almond extract
2 cups (12 ounces) semisweet
   chocolate chips
1 cup flaked coconut
1 cup sliced almonds

Mix the flour, baking soda, baking powder and salt together on waxed paper. Beat the butter, brown sugar and granulated sugar at medium speed in a large mixing bowl until creamy. Add the eggs, liqueur and almond extract and beat well. Beat in the flour mixture at low speed just until blended. Stir in the chocolate chips, coconut and almonds. Drop the dough by heaping tablespoonfuls 2 inches apart onto an ungreased large cookie sheet. Bake at 375 degrees for 10 to 12 minutes or until golden brown around the edges. Remove to wire racks to cool. Store in an airtight container for up to 1 week. **Makes 2 dozen.**

Contributed by Lisa Kick

Chocolate Cherry Macaroons

2 eggs
1/4 teaspoon salt
3/4 cup sugar
1/2 cup all-purpose flour
1 tablespoon shortening, butter or
    margarine, melted
1 teaspoon almond extract
1 (7-ounce) package flaked coconut
1 cup maraschino cherries, chopped
2 1/2 cups (15 ounces) semisweet chocolate chips

Beat the eggs and salt in a mixing bowl until frothy. Add the sugar gradually, beating constantly. Beat for 5 minutes or until thick and pale yellow. Stir in the flour, shortening and almond extract. Fold in the coconut, cherries and chocolate chips. Drop by teaspoonfuls onto greased cookie sheets. Bake at 325 degrees for 12 to 15 minutes or until brown. Remove to wire racks to cool. **Makes 4 dozen.**

Contributed by Jen Yohnka

Kieflies

12 ounces cream cheese, softened
2 cups (4 sticks) butter, softened
4 cups all-purpose flour
2 (12-ounce) cans or jars fruit pastry filling
   (sold in the baking section; this is not
   jelly or pie filling)
Confectioners' sugar

Beat the cream cheese in a mixing bowl for 2 minutes. Add the butter and beat for 2 minutes. Beat in the flour gradually and continue to beat for 2 minutes or until the mixture is smooth and the flour is mixed in completely. Divide the dough into 4 equal portions. Shape each portion into a ball and wrap separately in waxed paper. Chill for 6 to 10 hours. Roll one ball at a time into a thin but workable rectangle on a floured surface. Cut the rectangle into 2×2-inch squares. Place a small amount of the filling in the center of each square and pinch together the opposite corners to form a cookie. Place 1/2 inch apart on a cookie sheet. Bake at 350 degrees for 8 to 10 minutes or just until the edges turn light brown. The size and thickness of the cookie will determine the baking time. Be sure not to overfill or the filling will ooze out onto the cookie sheet. Cool the cookies on wire racks. Dust with confectioners' sugar when ready to serve. **Makes about 6 dozen.**

This is a traditional Polish cookie I have baked with my mom for many, many years. This recipe has been a part of our family and my mother's family for all of her 82 years. She continues to make them each year at Christmastime for our friends and family to share. Our favorite fillings include apricot, cherry, and pineapple. You can also use finely chopped nuts mixed with a small amount of sugar.

Contributed by Jane Koehler

If you want to lift yourself up, lift up someone else. —Booker T. Washington

Index

Index

Index

Index

great WOMEN, *great* FOOD

The Junior League of Kankakee County

To order, contact
The Junior League of Kankakee County
P. O. Box 365
Kankakee, Illinois 60901

Telephone
(815) 937-0877

Web site
www.jlkankakee.org